Alternative Development Strategies for Africa

VOLUME ONE
Coalition for Change

Contributors: B. Onimode, H. Sunmonu, H. Okullu,
B. Turok, E. Maganya, M. Turok, M. Suliman

Institute for African Alternatives (IFAA)

Alternative Development Strategies for Africa
Volume One: Coalition for Change was first published by
The Institute for African Alternatives, 23 Bevenden Street,
London N1 6BH, United Kingdom, in 1990.

Cover design by Step Forward Design
Typeset by Opus 43, Cumbria, UK
Printed and bound by Billings Book Plan

British Library Cataloguing in Publication Data
Alternative development strategies for Africa.
  Vol. 1 Coalition for change.
  1. Africa. Economic development
  I. Onimode, Bade   II. Institute for African Alternatives
  330.96

ISBN 1-870425-20-0

Contents

About the Contributors

DR BADE ONIMODE is Professor of Economics at the University of Ibadan, Nigeria, and a well-known author on the political economy of Africa. He chairs the Council of the Institute for African Alternatives (IFAA).

HASSAN SUNMONU is Secretary General of the Organization of African Trade Union Unity (OATUU) and has been prominent in debates on debt and development.

RT REVD J. HENRY OKULLU is Bishop of Maseno South, Kenya and an outspoken champion of human rights.

BEN TUROK is Director of the Institute for African Alternatives and has written extensively on Africa.

DR ERNEST MAGANYA is a lecturer in Economics at the Institute of Development Studies, Dar es Salaam University and an expert on structural adjustment.

MARY TUROK is a South African, a social worker and a feminist.

DR MOHAMED SULIMAN is Deputy Director of IFAA and Head of the Environment Unit. He was formerly a lecturer in Chemistry at the University of Khartoum, Sudan.

Acknowledgements

IFAA wishes to express its appreciation to the President of Tanzania, His Excellency Ali Hassan Mwinyi, for agreeing to open the Dar es Salaam Conference and for his support and encouragement. We wish to thank the Chief Minister of Zanzibar, Dr Omar Ali Juma, for closing the conference. Special thanks are due to Professor Haroub Othman for his untiring efforts as Convener of the Conference, the Institute of Development Studies for co-sponsoring the Conference with IFAA, and the University of Dar es Salaam for making all its facilities available to us so readily.

The Dar es Salaam Conference and the publication of its proceedings was made possible by the support received from Buntstift.e. V, Danchurch Aid, Misereor, Interchurch Aid Netherlands and Danida, to whom we are much indebted.

Abbreviations

AAF—SAP	African Alternative Framework to Structural Adjustment Programmes for Socio-Economic Recovery and Transformation
ACP	African, Caribbean and Pacific Countries
ADP	Agricultural Development Project
CAP	Common Agricultural Policy
CFA	Communauté Francaise Africaine
EEC	European Economic Community
ECA (UN)	Economic Commission for Africa
ECOWAS	Economic Community of West African States
ERP	Economic Recovery Programme
FAO	Food and Agricultural Organization
GATT	General Agreement on Tariffs and Trade
GDP	Gross Domestic Product
GNP	Gross National Product
ICC	Industrialized Capitalist Country
IDS	Institute of Development Studies (Univ. of Dar es Salaam)
IFAA	Institute for African Alternatives
ILO	International Labour Organization
IMF	International Monetary Fund
KANU	Kenyan African National Union
LIBOR	London Interbank Official Rate
MNC	multinational corporation
MULPOC	Multinational Programming Organization Centre
NAM	Non-Aligned Movement
NCCK	National Christian Council of Kenya
NIDL	New International Division of Labour
OAU	Organization of African Unity
OATUU	Organization of African Trade Union Unity
PASEC	Pacific Asian States Economic Cooperation
PTA	Preferential Trade Area for Eastern and Southern Africa
SADCC	Southern African Development Coordination Conference
SAP	Structural Adjustment Programme
SFEM	Second-Tier Foreign Exchange Market
SSA	Sub-Saharan Africa
UNDP	United Nations Development Programme
UNICEF	United Nations Children Fund
UNPF	United Nations Population Fund
UNTAG	United Nations Transitional Assistance Group
WHO	World Health Organization

Foreword

I would like to seize this opportunity to congratulate the Institute for African Alternatives on its very successful and timely conference — Alternative Development Strategies for Africa — and on the publication of the conference proceedings in three volumes. This is a great service to our beleaguered continent, and one that I commend very strongly to other African non-governmental organizations. For us at ECA, it is always a pleasure and a source of inspiration to know and co-operate with organizations and other bodies that promote Africa's development interests.

In this regard it is well to recollect the nature of the African crisis to which this conference addresses its proposed Alternative Development Strategies. As ECA has been emphasizing for many a year, this is not only an economic crisis, but also a political, social and human crisis of immense proportions. Starting with an agrarian crisis and increasing food deficit in the 1970s, it rapidly deteriorated by the 1980s into a deep depression compounded by an external debt crisis and a serious refugee problem. These have been exacerbated by the disastrous failure of IMF—World Bank supported Structural Adjustment Programmes (SAPs), as reflected vividly in this year's World Bank Report on *World Poverty* which shows alarmingly that Africa will be the only region in the world where per capita income will continue to fall right up to the twenty-first century.

While internal factors like domestic policy failures, unproductive investment, economic mismanagement, natural disasters such as drought during 1983/85, etc. have contributed to the crisis, the dominant causes have been external. These external factors include the collapse of Africa's commodity exports in the 1980s, the sharply deteriorating external lending conditions, the depression in the advanced countries in the last decade, the activities of international financial institutions and other transnationals as well as the overall deterioration of the international economic environment.

All these pose special challenges to African scholars, non-governmental organizations and all other Africans for the resolution of the crisis. As I have stated repeatedly, Europeans developed Europe, Americans transformed America and the Japanese developed Japan, and so, only the Africans themselves can develop Africa. We can only be assisted by our foreign development partners. Hence Africans at all levels of our societies must rise to the challenge and assume their historic responsibility. Thus we must realize that even if all Africa's external debts are written off today and nothing else is done, the debt crisis will recur in a few years. African scholars and others must, therefore, mobilize themselves urgently to articulate and implement alternative programmes, strategies and policies for transformation in all aspects of African economy and society — economic sectors, politics and democracy, social structures and values, women and meso policies. We must also collectively resist the growing marginalization of Africa and its crippling foreign domination which undermine the sovereignty of African countries and the dignity of the Africans.

It is in order to galvanize, guide and support these regional initiatives that the ECA has been elaborating and canvassing alternative programmes, policy directions and policy measures over the years. These major initiatives include the preparation of the Lagos Plan of Action in 1980 for the pursuit of a collective, self-reliant development strategy in Africa; the African Priority Programme for Economic Recovery during 1986—90, which was adopted by the United Nations as the United Nations Programme of Action for African Economic Recovery and Development, and the more recent launching of the African Alternative Framework to Structural Adjustment Programmes for Socio-Economic Recovery and Transformation (AAF—SAP) in July 1989. The in-depth studies of selected major policy instruments like multiple exchange rates, differential interest rates and selective credit control, as well as price support policies for regional food self-sufficiency, have been completed for the operationalization of AAF–SAP.

The major thrust of this African alternative to ongoing orthodox SAPs is the simultaneous pursuit of adjustment with the accelerated structural transformation of African economies. This calls for alternative policy directions such as the strengthening and diversification of production, human-centred development, the creation of an enabling environment for transformation that involves the full democratization of African societies through popular participation by all, especially women, and effective market and production integration in Africa, among others. The fact must be underlined that only through collective action can Africa resolve its protracted crisis, and this requires transcending the erstwhile illusion of independent national development in a continent of fragmented markets and minuscule states.

It is my sincere hope that IFAA and other African organizations will sustain their support for alternative development in Africa through the translation of the laudable recommendations contained in these conference proceedings into concrete activities on the ground. This will require the mounting of sustained support for African countries to design and implement their own alternative programmes for recovery and transformation.

The multilateral financial institutions and the rest of the international community should, therefore, be pressured to provide adequate export opportunities, external debt relief, and financial and technical support for African countries to implement these alternative development strategies urgently.

Adebayo Adedeji
United Nations Under-Secretary-General
and Executive Secretary of the Economic
Commission for Africa

The Search for Solutions

His Excellency President Ali Hassan Mwinyi*

---

* Read on his behalf by Professor Kighoma Malima, Minister of State in the President's Office and Vice-Chairman of the National Planning Commission.

diagnosis of any malaise is the foundation of an appropriate cure. A plan for overcoming it. Thus, I cannot overemphasize the need to identify the real cause of Africa's economic problems in order to be able to propose appropriate measures for their correction.

The holding of this conference reinforces my long-held view that the search for solutions to Africa's economic problems cannot, and in fact should not, be the responsibility of politicians and government officials alone. It is, indeed, the responsibility of everyone, especially of our experts in the public sector, the private sector and the academic institutions. Thus I am greatly encouraged to see such eminent persons, from both within and outside Tanzania, gathered here to discuss Alternative Development Strategies for Africa. I would, therefore, like to express my deep appreciation to both the Institute of Development Studies (IDS) of the University of Dar es Salaam and the Institute for African Alternatives (IFAA) for organizing this conference on a subject which is extremely relevant to current concerns and efforts to reverse the economic decline in our continent.

I am sure one of the questions you will ask yourselves during your discussions is why Africa today is in such a state of economic decline in spite of the post-independence enthusiasm of its people and leaders. That question is pertinent because a correct diagnosis of any malaise is the foundation of an appropriate prescription for overcoming it. Thus, I cannot overemphasize the need to identify the real cause of Africa's economic plight in order to be able to propose appropriate strategies for overcoming it. The problem we often face, however, is that there are as many different interpretations of our economic problems as there are proposals for solving them.

3

For example, no doubt you are aware of the persistent claims made by our critics that the main cause of Africa's economic problems is the Africans themselves, especially their leaders and their inappropriate policies. Indeed, I would be dishonest if I denied that we Africans have made mistakes in our efforts to meet the post-independence twin challenge of bringing about the economic development of our countries as well as improving the living standards of our people. We have made mistakes — albeit with good intentions — and we have been courageous enough to admit them openly.

Some of you may recall, for instance, that at the Twenty-First OAU Summit in 1985, African heads of state acknowledged that inadequate structures contributed to the economic difficulties now confronting our continent. They specifically pointed out in their declaration that national development plans and annual budgets of most African countries have tended to perpetuate and even accentuate the dependency of our economies through over-reliance on both financial and human resources from outside. Furthermore, those plans and budgets have often led to misallocation of resources, taking the form of reduced shares to such high-priority sectors as agriculture, industry, education and manpower development. The massive expenditure on foreign consumer goods and non-productive investment projects was another manifestation of the underlying defect.

What is interesting is that, in spite of what are regarded as our internal shortcomings, the economies of most African countries made notable progress in the 1960s and the early 1970s. There was, in particular, a remarkable expansion of basic social services such as health, education and clean water. New physical infrastructures such as roads and railways were built and old ones improved. Moreover, during that period, the GDP of African countries also increased annually at an average rate of about 6 per cent, compared to the growth rate of about 3 per cent in 1988.

Such impeccable evidence makes it obvious that internal shortcomings cannot be wholly responsible for the economic deterioration currently taking place in our continent. It is, after all, the same people of Africa and, except for minor modifications, the same policies which contributed to the expansion of social services and economic growth in the 1960s and the early 1970s. In some cases, the leaders who propelled the economic and social advances of the 1960s and early 1970s were the same ones who had the bitter experience of helplessly witnessing those gains being eroded by factors beyond their control. The economic ills facing Africa today do, in any case, cut across political as well as ideological boundaries. Besides, it is neither reasonable nor rational to imagine that the leaders and policy-makers of Africa have willingly decided, in the 1980s, to mismanage their economies.

Thus it becomes absolutely necessary to examine the great impact on Africa's economies of those external factors over which we have no control. Those factors, especially the ones emanating from the negative changes in the international economic climate, have indeed dealt a very severe blow to our development efforts.

It is a well-known fact that the reasonable economic performance which occurred in Africa during the 1960s and early 1970s was sustained through foreign exchange earnings from export commodities. Those export earnings were supplemented by official development assistance as well as private capital inflows from the developed countries. However, from the mid-1970s the situation began to change dramatically.

The most dramatic change took place in the international trading environment. In the industrialized countries, for instance, the demand for our export commodities began to decline sharply and that precipitated the collapse of international commodity prices. It is estimated that real commodity prices have been declining at an annual average rate of 10 per cent. The situation has drastically reduced our foreign exchange earnings and, consequently, our capacity to import, which had played the major role in sustaining the reasonable post-independence economic performance. Thus, as a result of the persistent deterioration of the terms of trade of most African countries during the period from 1980 to 1986, for instance, Africa's export earnings dropped from more than 90 billion to only 50 billion US dollars.

It is equally ominous that prospects for an expansion of commodity trade are being made slim by four main factors. First, there is a change in consumption patterns in the developed countries. That change has reduced the demand for our agricultural commodities. Secondly, the substitution of synthetic materials for natural raw materials continues to depress the demand for such primary commodities as sisal and cotton. Thirdly, the demand for raw materials has been adversely affected by rapid technological progress in the developed countries. As a result of that development, less raw material and other inputs are now required per unit of final product. Fourthly, in their efforts to protect their economies, the industrialized countries — the very architects of liberal trade — have abandoned the rules of free trade by resorting increasingly to protectionist measures against both primary as well as manufactured and semi-manufactured products of African and other developing countries.

The deterioration in the terms of trade, and the consequent reduction in export earnings and capacity to import, were not the only external factors which reversed Africa's economic growth. I mentioned earlier that Africa's post-independence development momentum was sustained by both commodity export earnings, supplemented by official development assistance from the developed countries. Unfortunately, as export earnings dwindled because of the collapse of commodity prices, African countries also became victims of the so-called 'aid fatigue' which swept across the donor community.

Thus, the terms of foreign aid became harder as contending parties in the donor countries increasingly questioned the validity of continuing to assist the poor to help themselves. Issues such as those relating to human rights were included among the conditions for receiving foreign economic assistance. As a result of the growing aid fatigue, only a few developed countries have so far met the target set by the United Nations that the developed countries should transfer 0.7 per cent of their Gross National Product (GNP) to the developing countries in the form of official development assistance.

Furthermore, environmental issues are among the latest conditions for securing loans from international financial institutions. I am not suggesting in any way that environmental protection should not be given the attention it deserves in our efforts to promote sustainable economic development in our continent. The dangers of desertification caused by over-cultivation and over-grazing are all too familiar to us. I know, for example, that as the price of kerosene, which is widely used as a source of energy for cooking in our continent, continues to rise, more and more people resort to firewood and charcoal. That situation undoubtedly increases the dangers of deforestation and desertification which would aggravate the already miserable living conditions in Africa.

We all see the link between economic development and environmental protection. What is incomprehensible is the growing tendency to blame the poor countries for the degradation of the environment while the same countries are victims of the dumping of industrial toxic waste by the developed countries. It sounds particularly odd to force the poor to slow down their pace of development for the sake of protecting the environment, while the developed countries continue with such dangerous actions as testing nuclear weapons, industrial pollution, excessive use of fossil fuels and even dumping toxic waste on the shores of our continent and elsewhere.

It is important to bear in mind that because of today's great scientific and technological achievements, the world we live in has been reduced to a single village. What takes place in one part of the world can have a catastrophic effect on all mankind. Therefore, environmental problems should be considered and tackled in a global context. The poor and rich countries alike should strive to work together closely in order to protect and preserve the global environment in the same concerted manner that has become the hallmark of our efforts to combat terrorism and AIDS for the benefit of all mankind.

Indeed, the list of external factors which retard Africa's economic growth and development would be incomplete without an examination of the debt problem. The problem often receives scant attention because Africa's debt is not big enough to pose a threat to the international financial system. Nevertheless, we can legitimately ask ourselves how a continent whose annual export earnings amount to just about 50 billion US dollars, could possibly service an external debt amounting to more than 230 billion dollars without starving our people as well as causing political and social turmoil in our respective countries?

There is no doubt that the problem persists and debt-servicing continues to consume Africa's valuable resources, badly needed to even maintain minimum living conditions for our people. In fact, the combination of deteriorating terms of trade and debt-servicing have triggered a reverse transfer of real resources from the poor to the rich countries. Thus, the debt problem is a real obstacle to Africa's efforts towards achieving economic recovery and sustained development.

I have mentioned some of the external factors which inhibit our progress in order to illustrate that the development of our countries requires more than hard work from our people or good management by African governments. I have not even mentioned the horror and misery caused by such natural disasters as floods, droughts and famine which have hit many African countries in recent years. It is, therefore, a combination of all those factors, with the unfavourable international economic environment playing a pivotal role, which has eroded our capacity not only to implement development programmes, but even to sustain the essential social services built during the post-independence era.

Consequently, the much expanded health services in many African countries are cramped for lack of equipment and medicine, while schools do not have sufficient teaching aids and books, not to mention desks for primary schools. The newly built and inherited physical infrastructures such as roads and railways have also deteriorated for lack of spares and appropriate maintenance.

Our own experience, here in Tanzania, adequately illustrates the severity of the impact of external factors on our efforts to achieve economic recovery and sustained growth. As is well known, our enthusiasm to implement the multilaterally funded Economic Recovery Programme (ERP) was met with partial success. The reason why that success was only partial is not that our people did not work hard. On the contrary, the people of Tanzania responded positively and worked very hard in support of the ERP.

Our farmers, in particular, deserve our heartfelt commendation for their exemplary contribution. We were equally blessed to have received sufficient rains during the whole period of the ERP. The efforts of the farmers and the good rains we received enabled us to increase substantially both food and cash crop production. That positive development was instrumental in improving, to a very considerable extent, the food situation in the country.

We had hoped that the substantial increase in cash crop production would also increase our export earnings and hence ease our acute foreign exchange shortage. But once again our hopes were shattered by the unfavourable world trading system, especially the collapse of international commodity prices. Consequently, while the production of cotton, for example, increased from 200,000 bales in 1985/86 to more than 460,000 bales in 1987/88, the world price of cotton declined, in the same period, from 68 US cents per pound to only 34 US cents. The story is not any different as far as the prices of our other export commodities like coffee, are concerned.

The loss we incurred as a result of the sharp fall in the prices of our export commodities was aggravated by the requirement to part with scarce and desperately needed foreign exchange resources for the purpose of debt-servicing. In spite of the partial rescheduling achieved through the Paris Club agreement, we still had to pay, as debt service, 388 million US dollars in 1987/88 alone. The amount would have been even larger if we had met all our obligations under that agreement. Thus, the loss of such critical foreign exchange, caused by the decline in commodity prices as well as debt servicing, was a genuine obstacle to the success of the ERP.

Similarly, it became increasingly clear during the course of the implementation of the ERP that some of the IMF's conditions did not fully take into account the particular needs of our country. Instead of putting greater emphasis on the real bottlenecks such as an inadequate transport system and insufficient processing capacity, we were subjected to the standard prescriptions such as credit ceiling, producer prices and massive devaluation. Some of those conditions have proved to be counter-productive to the hard work and great sacrifices made by our people.

The massive devaluation of our currency, for example, has led to a very sharp increase in the imports of machinery, spares, raw materials, fertilizers and insecticides which are needed to sustain increased production. Devaluation has also greatly eroded the purchasing power of the people, especially those in the low-income brackets. In short, some of the conditions undermine our commitment to promote and protect the interests of the most disadvantaged people in our society. Sometimes one gets the impression that the prescriptions imposed on the recipient countries are not completely free from the ideological preferences of the donor countries.

That impression or feeling compels us to draw certain conclusions. The most obvious of them all is that Africa will not be developed by foreign assistance because, first, such assistance is on the decline and is becoming more unpredictable. But more fundamentally, and even more disturbingly, the conditions for foreign aid are getting harder as well as more politicized. If that trend continues, and there is every indication that it will, the outcome would be to undermine greatly our ability to follow a development strategy of our own choice, which takes fully into account the aspirations of our people. That is why the Arusha Declaration warned us, as long ago as 1967, that independence cannot be real if a nation depends excessively upon gifts and loans from others for its development.

I cannot, therefore, over-emphasize the obvious fact that the time has come for us to translate our policy of self-reliance into action. We must depend more and more on our own resources and develop their potential. No one can deny the fact that, apart from the vast natural resources, Africa's greatest resource is its people. So whatever development strategy we choose to adopt, it must ensure the maximum participation of our people in the resultant development process.

African countries can also face the twin challenge of survival and development through increased cooperation among themselves as well as enhancing their capacity for collective self-reliance. The efforts being made by SADCC and PTA member countries will greatly strengthen cooperation and economic integration in the sub-region. Indeed, it is through such sub-regional cooperation and integration that Africa can possibly overcome the developmental handicaps associated with an inadequate resource base and limited market opportunities imposed by the national frontiers.

At the global level, African countries should continue to work closely together with other developing countries, in order to strengthen their case and to struggle for the establishment of a more equitable and just world economic order. The success of that struggle will create a more favourable world economic environment which would be more conducive to the development efforts of African and other developing countries.

Distinguished participants, the enormity of the task confronting the African continent can hardly be overstated. I am confident, however, that the potential exists within Africa itself to enable the continent to extricate itself from its present plight. What is needed is an appropriate development strategy that would ensure the maximum exploitation of that potential for the benefit of Africa and its people. I do hope, therefore, that this conference will come up with implementable as well as realistic and relevant recommendations, which would enable us to formulate an appropriate development strategy for our continent.

INTRODUCTION

Alternative Development Path for Africa — A Macro Framework

Bade Onimode

The sheer enormity and intensification of the African crisis that has made the 1980s a lost decade for the continent underscores the urgent imperative of an alternative development path for the region. Disastrous economic performance over years is always an indication of inappropriate development strategies. Hence we must insist that the persistence and deterioration of the African crisis into a catastrophe is eloquent proof of the bankruptcy of current Structural Adjustment Programmes (SAPs) or Economic Recovery Programmes (ERPs) in Africa. With some fifteen African countries on the verge of economic collapse, with rapidly contracting economies, the pervasive collapse of the welfare state and widespread starvation, the objective necessity for the age of alternatives in Africa is obvious.

The current campaign to resolve the unbearable external debt crisis also warrants alternative strategies. The basic point here is that if all external debts were cancelled or repudiated now, and other things were to remain the same, then in another five years or so there would be another debt crisis. This underscores the need for supplementing efforts at foreign debt resolution with the simultaneous elaboration of alternative strategies for organizing and operating the African economy. This is why as part of the current debt campaign the Economic Commission for Africa (ECA) has designed *AAF—SAP* (*African Alternative Framework to Structural Adjustment Programmes for Socio-Economic Recovery and Transformation*) as the relevant alternative to the orthodox SAPs that have failed so woefully.

The approach of the Fourth UN Development Decade of the 1990s and its International Development Strategy[1] also requires the design of different regional development strategies. This is critical against the background of the non-fulfilment of the main objectives of the first three UN Development Decades since 1960. In particular, the poor performance of the UN Industrial Decade for Africa (the 1980s), food and rural development strategies, etc., as well as the basic lack of mobilization around the Third UN Decade, all dictate the need for re-thinking and re-orientation towards the forthcoming International Development Strategy. These are especially critical in view of the emergent restructuring of the world economy in the 1990s.

Perspectives of African Development

Besides thematic pre-occupations such as debt and adjustment, the role of transnational corporations in Africa, participation of women, politics and democracy, etc., it is essential to focus on a holistic, systematic framework that aggregates the specific strategies for different themes into a general macro-perspective. This is to coordinate the specialized strategies within an overall orientation that gives general direction and charts the trajectory for the African economy in the short, medium and long terms. Apart from the spirited endeavours of individual researchers and groups, three different but general perspectives of Africa's development have been produced by the ECA and the World Bank. These consist of the ECA's AAF—SAP and its longer-term study titled *Beyond Recovery — ECA's Revised Perspectives of Africa's Development, 1990—2008* [2] as well as the World Bank's recent *Sub-Saharan Africa: from Crisis to Sustainable Growth — a Long-Term Perspective Study.*

All of them address the challenges of Africa's long-term structural transformation, though AAF—SAP combines this development orientation with the requirements of current recovery. It has been designed specifically as a concrete alternative to orthodox SAPs and its central thrust is that recovery and structural transformation must proceed simultaneously and not sequentially as in orthodox adjustment programmes. This is to ensure that the search for financial stability in the short run in orthodox SAPs does not destroy the basis for growth and development by undermining the development of human resources, industry, agriculture, food and African integration. The alternative in AAF-SAP is thus derived from the basic objectives of the *Lagos Plan of Action* which are the achievement of (a) regional food self-sufficiency — not just food security, which can be attained through foreign aid that may be withdrawn as a political weapon; (b) satisfaction of critical needs for shelter, health care, housing, etc. for the alleviation of mass poverty; (c) sustained growth and development; (d) national and collective self-reliance to terminate the prostrate external dependence of African countries.

Another major strength of AAF—SAP is its commitment to the broad democratization of African societies. This is part of the enabling environment that it recommends for the achievement of rapid recovery and transformation. This popular participation in decision-making over the allocation of resources and the distribution of the benefits of development at all levels is critical for effective mobilization of resources, resistance to persistently subversive foreign intervention in Africa and the implementation of policies and programmes. This democratization also includes the effective participation of women in the recovery and development process. AAF—SAP is, however, not a programme on the ground, but a holistic framework for designing specific country programmes.

AAF—SAP is thus linked organically to ECA's *Revised Perspectives*. Both derive from the long-term development objectives of the *Lagos Plan of Action* so that AAF—SAP can be regarded as the short- and medium-term components of the *Revised Perspectives*. The *Revised Perspectives* consist of two scenarios — a projection of the historical trend and a normative scenario. The projection of the historical trend of the African economy yields such politicaliy unacceptable results as population growth from 544 million in 1986 to 1,070 million by the year 2008, GDP growth rate of only 2.6 per cent annually for 1990–2008 with implied per capita income decline of 0.7 per cent yearly, agricultural decline of 0.1 per cent per annum, investment fall of 4 per cent annually, export decline of 4.2 per cent per annum and a deterioration of current account deficit from $3.6 billion in 1985 to $41.9 billion by year 2008.[3]

In the normative scenario, population growth rate per annum is projected to fall from around 3.3 to 2.7 per cent, with the GDP growing at 5.7 per cent annually so that per capita income can double by the year 2008 at about 2 to 3 per cent annual growth rate. Food self-sufficiency is to be attained and industrial output is to grow at 9 per cent annually during 1990–2008, slightly above the Lima target of the UN. Intra-African trade is to rise from the current low level of around 5 per cent to 25 per cent of Africa's total trade while the current account deficit is to fall from the $41.9 billion of the historical trend to $16.7 billion with improvements in the international commodity and financial environment.[4] Apart from these aggregate and sectoral economic projections, for official sectoral balances, the normative scenario also calls for a *new social order*. This is anchored to the democratization of the development process in economic, political and social terms. Basic needs are to be satisfied for all and popular participation of all social groups is to be ensured as part of an enabling environment. This involves the cultivation of an appropriate system of values, general education, and the development of social institutions around cooperation and African norms. The preliminary study for ECA's long-term perspective was published in 1983 and *Revised Perspectives* is to be published in 1990.

Possible improvements to the ECA's long-term perspective are the expansion of its socio-political component, its conversion from an official into a political document and its translation into national programmes in African countries.

The political and social dimensions of the normative scenario can be expanded with respect to forms of popular participation, modalities for democratization, especially at grassroots level, and the envisaged social structure. To ensure that *Revised Perspectives* does not just remain on shelves, it should be made a political document that is widely disseminated and debated throughout Africa. In this way, people and governments can become committed to its implementation by knowing about it and seeing how it embraces their aspirations as individuals, groups and countries. This leads directly to the need for African governments to prepare parallel long-term programmes or perspectives for their national development. This is the concrete way in which the *Revised Perspectives* can become operationally binding on individual countries. Even though it is possible that current medium-term programmes in some countries relate to the ECA's long-term perspectives, it is still necessary for these countries to design long-term or perspective plans in order to ensure effective consistency and coordination with the ECA's perspectives.

The third major perspective of African development is the World Bank's recent publication *From Crisis to Sustainable Growth*. Unlike the failed IMF-World Bank SAP (or ERP) and the World Bank's discredited Berg Report (*Towards Accelerated Development in Sub-Saharan Africa*), this new effort has commendable features. It shows some convergence with the ECA's position as regards human-centred development, sustainable growth with equity, socio-political dimensions of transformation, and support for African integration (opposed by the Berg Report).

But the World Bank's perspective also has serious shortcomings. With regard to agriculture, it has an objective of food security rather than regional food self-sufficiency as demanded by African countries; its projected annual growth rate is only 4 to 5 per cent as against the ECA's 5.7 per cent; and its new generation SAPs are to be based on essentially the same unsatisfactory performance criteria of exports, GDP growth, exchange rate, inflation, etc. as the orthodox adjustment programmes. The human-centred development is also to be based on cost recovery and subsidy reduction, while the seven themes of the Bank's 'strategic agenda for the 1990s' are silent on external debt, food agriculture, industrialization and population. Similarly, the Bank's incrementalist conception of African integration — in barely fourteen of the book's 300 pages — reads like an afterthought or footnote, and ignores the major *production* aspects of integration such as industrialization, agriculture, technology and construction. Finally, as the whole of Africa is in crisis, the Bank's long-term perspective should have been developed for the continent as a whole and not just its sub-Saharan region.

The Global Context of Africa's Future Development

In an interdependent world that is demanding solidarity for development and peace, it is clear that African development necessarily occurs in a global context. That has, indeed, always been the case. What is problematic, however, is the under-standing of that international environment, the anticipation of its major changes and the effective reconciliation of its interests with those of Africa — to the extent that this is feasible.

These issues take on a grave significance on account of the shattering experiences of the 1980s in particular, and the past in general, and in view of clearly misplaced faith in the neutrality and benevolence of the external environment. As the inter-national environment has become more hostile with talk of 'aid fatigue', some have even been saying openly that the rest of the world owes Africa nothing. That, of course, is true neither literally nor politically. We all belong to this planet and must share its resources and this is why the notion of 'Africa's development partners' remains current — even outside the UN system. But we must not romanticize the external environment of the region's transformation — the global context should be faced realistically and evaluated continuously. This is particularly critical on the threshold of the 1990s.

Parallels between the 1940s and the 1990s

Historical parallels have been drawn between the 1930s and 1980s. Both decades witnessed a global depression and an international debt crisis, though that of the 1930s was confined to Latin America. In both decades, the economic crisis started in the industrialized capitalist countries and spilled over into the Third World countries through their external sector. But the Great Depression of 1929—33 was deeper and more destructive of national capitals than the current one, which has been a longer crisis, especially on the periphery.

In the succeeding decades, both crises led or are leading to fundamental restructuring of the world economy. After the 1930s, the following decade hosted the Bretton Woods economic and monetary system from 1944. The crisis of the 1980s is also likely to be followed in the 1990s by fundamental regional changes in the world economy. Besides the spectacular shift of economic and political power from Western Europe and North America to Pacific Asia, there is detente between East and West together with dramatic reforms in the socialist world and a major realignment of the world economy into three huge trading blocs. The North American bloc combining the US and Canada now has a Free Trade Area and may develop into a full Economic Community. Its major external preoccupation will be Latin America. After 1992 the second bloc, Europe, will be concerned mainly with Eastern Europe in a possible bid to build a Greater Europe. A Pacific Asian bloc is also in the making through the Pacific Asian States Economic Cooperation (PASEC); its preoccupation will be the rest of Asia.

The involuntary delinking of Africa

This scenario depicts an emergent world economy of the 1990s that will be restructured into dominant economic blocs with respective regional interests that all exclude Africa. In particular, the birth of Europe in 1992 may be expected to marginalize and weaken the Lomé Convention between the EEC and the ACP (African, Caribbean and Pacific) countries. This means that the difficulties and near stalemate in the negotiations over Lome IV (to come into operation from 1990), which has been subjected to conditionality and structural adjustment like Lome III (1987), are ominous forebodings of the likely fate of the Lome Convention. For example, with the establishment of the European Monetary System c. 1992, the support of the French franc for the Francophone CFA is likely to disappear, and that will greatly weaken the CFA and its owners.

The special preferences enjoyed by ACP countries in the EEC and other countries for the export of primary commodities are also likely to disappear in the 1990s. The Uruguay Round of trade negotiations on GATT (General Agreement on Tariffs and Trade) has also been facing increasing difficulties,in particular since last year. These adverse developments mean that African commodity exports will have to face stiffer competition from Latin America and Asia, and even from Europe and the US. Yet, while the EEC subsidizes its agriculture under the Common Agricultural Policy (CAP) and the US does the same under its massive agricultural support programme, these same countries forbid African countries to maintain subsidies.

Then there is the rapidly falling demand for raw materials, due to two main factors: technical progress that has reduced the raw material content of manufacturing by some 30 per cent in the recent past, and growing protectionism spearheaded by the Reagan administration in the US. The combined effect of growing synthetic substitution for raw materials and rising protectionism is the sharply falling demand for Africa's raw material exports — which other Third World countries also face. The International Coffee Agreement has also collapsed — yet the World Bank preaches blanket export promotion. On the capital account of international trade, capital flows to Africa have also been dwindling or stagnant. Thus Africa's share of direct foreign investment in developing countries in the 1980s has hovered around 10 per cent. The flow of development assistance has also been poor, checked by the growing complaint of 'aid fatigue'.

The picture that emerges is that of an African region facing the grim prospects of involuntary de-linking from the world economy in the 1990s. The projection of the historical trend of this global scenario is politically unacceptable. There is thus an urgent need for a radical departure from these developments so that Africa can arrest some of them and utilize others as challenges for its recovery and transformation. It is against this harsh background that the macro framework sketched below has been elaborated for the articulation of alternative development strategies for Africa.

Alternative Development Path for Africa

The major objectives of Africa's alternative development strategy are both economic and socio-political. The basic economic goals correspond to those elaborated in AAF–SAP, the *Lagos Plan of Action* and the ECA's *Revised Perspectives* as stated earlier. But these economic objectives must be supplemented with political and social goals in the general drive to create a new social order or new social formation in African countries.

Objectives

The creation of a new social formation or new social order in Africa requires a new political culture — a new set of values and beliefs that regulate the process of government, the exercise of power and authority as well as basic attitudes to the state and authority. The major thrust of this new political culture is to arrest the persuasive lack of democracy and accountability so manifest in the authoritarianism and massive political repression on the continent. Here it has to be re-emphasized that without democracy and accountability there can be no development. Hence the main requirements for the creation of the new political culture are genuine democracy, effective accountability of leadership at all levels and politically responsive and humane leadership. These require genuine popular and grassroots participation in decision-making and the allocation of resources at all levels of society, effective community empowerment and the coordinated decentralization of decision-making and development processes.

The social goals that should complement these objectives are anchored to social justice, the work ethos, and the creation of an alternative system of values. These should replace persuasive materialism and morbid greed with African humanism, a permissive consumption ethos with a work ethos centred round the dignity of labour, and destructive competition for power and wealth with an approach which emphasizes cooperation. All these require the equitable distribution of income, wealth, power and social opportunities as well as the strengthening of social institutions like the family (both the traditional extended and the modern nuclear versions), cooperatives and popular organizations. The need for social harmony is central to all these and this requires (1) deliberate and creative policies to ameliorate the growing polarization of social classes through the rapid strengthening of oppressed classes and of social strata e.g., women, peasants and workers; and (2) the diffusion of ethno-religious cleavages. Happily the *Khartoum Declaration*[5] and the increasing commitment to human-centred development are turning attention to these critical political and social goals of African development. The point cannot be overemphasized that without the peace and social harmony that these socio-political goals generate, even with conflict of class interest, the *enabling environment* for development will not materialize.

Strategic choices for African development

The achievement of the major economic, political and social objectives of alternative development in Africa also requires the making of some strategic choices for the 1990s and beyond. These are mainly three, as follows:

1   Planned disengagement v involuntary de-linking;
2   African integration v global regrouping;
3   Demographic imperative v population explosion.

PLANNED DISENGAGEMENT OR INVOLUNTARY DE-LINKING

This debate is not new but the choice is now urgent. Here the issue is not whether Africa should head for autarky in a world of global interdependence. Given the emerging involuntary de-linking of Africa from the world economy, the real question is what Africa can do to ensure its collective survival and development. The answer is the strengthening of an existing commitment to inward-looking development within the strategy of national and collective self-reliance, which is essentially structural disengagement. It calls for primary reliance on Africa's own internal resources and energies rather than the past and current dependence on the external environment. Within this framework, African countries should still export and import, and engage in international capital dealings, but these should be subordinate to national and intra-African endeavours. Emerging realities do not leave Africa such choice. Where Africa has comparative advantages, they should be exploited to the fullest, but *not* in the naive way of just pushing traditional exports of raw materials and relying on foreign aid — even for food.

AFRICAN INTEGRATION AND GLOBAL RESTRUCTURING

The emerging economic blocs of the 1990s demand urgent collective action at the political and economic levels from Africa. These global developments, the external crisis and the structural adjustment approach of the IMF and the World Bank must be seen for the clear *political strategy* that they are. The overall objective of this international political strategy is to keep Africa down and out of world affairs and recolonize its economy. Africa requires a counter political strategy of urgent *concerted political action* on debt, SAPs and regional integration. African countries should refuse to negotiate individually with the advanced countries on these issues. The region's greatest strength lies in its effective political and economic unity. So Africa should develop its common position on foreign debt into an *African debtors' cartel* and link up with Latin American and Asian debtors' cartels to bargain effectively with the creditor cartels in the Club of London, Club of Paris and Group of Seven.

Then three levels of integration should be pursued: sub-regional, regional and South-South. At the sub-regional level, existing structures of integration such as Economic Community of West African States (ECOWAS), Preferential Trade Area for Eastern and Southern Africa (PTA), South African Development Coordination Conference (SADCC), etc. and their corresponding Multinational Programming Organization Centres (MULPOCs) need urgent revamping and strengthening. The rhetoric behind their creation should be translated urgently into serious policy actions of free trade, common tariffs, joint industrial and transport developments and similar ventures. Parallel or conflicting cooperative structures, especially among francophone countries, that impede these integrative arrangements should be rationalized urgently. French interference with these sub-regional groupings should also be exposed and neutralized systematically.

Then overall regional or intra-African integration should be speeded up in three main directions. First, the immense opportunities for barter trade among African countries should be studied by the ECA and OAU at regular intervals and the results and mechanisms should be disseminated widely among African countries and their Chambers of Commerce. This is one sure way of relaxing the foreign exchange constraint on intra-African trade. Uganda is positively engaging in this barter trade with Libya and that should be expanded and emulated by other African countries. Sub-regional trade by barter should also be encouraged. Second, the date for the realization of the African Common Market which is planned for the period 2000 to 2008 should be advanced. The protocol of agreement for a Common Market should be signed early in the 1990s and its implementation should be completed by the year 2000. Then the African Economic Community should be established towards 2000 and its implementation completed by 2010. Third, monetary integration at both sub-regional and regional levels should also be pushed systematically. An encouraging development in this respect is the creation of the PTA travellers' cheque — its wider acceptability should be encouraged by the member governments and their Central Banks. The current efforts on trade payments and clearing houses among African countries should be encouraged by member governments so that with the declining support of the Francophone CFA by the French franc from around 1992, African monetary integration should be well advanced.

The politics of integration is central to all these points. The promotion of common languages among African countries, such as the use of Swahili in Eastern Africa, is important for improving the communication required for intra-African cooperation. The teaching of French and Portuguese in non-Francophone and non-Luxophone African countries would also assist and so would the wider teaching of such African languages as Lingala in Central Africa and of Hansa, Yoruba and Wollo in West and Central Africa. Joint education will also promote effective intra-African communication and cooperation; so will sub-regional and regional trade fairs (e.g., the PTA leather show in Addis Ababa in December 1989), agricultural and air shows as well as intra-African television and radio programmes.

South-South cooperation around the Non-Aligned Movement (NAM) should also complement African integrative efforts. The emphasis at the last summit of the NAM on cooperation with respect to foreign debt and the West is a salutary development in this regard. But the South Commission should also be invigorated by member states through better funding, barter trade, greater publicity and popular mobilization around its activities, as well as the expansion of joint ventures in manufacturing, technology, etc.

THE DEMOGRAPHIC IMPERATIVE IN AFRICAN DEVELOPMENT

Africa must urgently and more seriously tackle the demographic context of its development. An annual population growth rate of around 3.3 per cent, which is the highest in the world, is unsustainable with the projected annual decline of agriculture of 0.1 per cent. The 50 per cent of young dependents (under fourteen years) is also too high. It should be emphasized here that the three basic demographic problems in Africa are the excessively high rate of population growth, the excessive proportion of young and old dependents and the maldistribution of the existing population. It is no use suggesting in this regard that slow economic growth is the real problem because even if the rate of economic growth was to rise to around 5.7 per cent (the projected normative rate), the current growth rate of the population would still not permit much improvement in living standards. This is why even though the Chinese have been enjoying an annual growth rate of 6 to 9 per cent annually over several years, they have also been keeping their population growth rate much lower than 3.3 per cent annually. The average number of children per woman, which currently hovers around 7 in Africa, should fall drastically to around 4 or 5 by the end of the century.

Organized migration should redistribute the population from high density to low density zones in order to ease the growing problems of landlessness. The development of rural areas and the ending of the anti-rural bias of official policy is central to this in order to limit rural-urban migration. Effective land reform measures are also critical to this spatial redistribution of the population. The unsatisfactory demographic structure of African countries, with over 70 per cent of the population as dependents in the age cohorts of 0—14 and over 65, is also very unsatisfactory. This high dependency ratio diminishes the level of participation in production and exerts a downward trend on living standards through excessive consumption and social service expenditures for food, housing, education, health, etc. A lowering of the birth rate reduces the 0—14 age cohort and increases the proportion of the active population.

Alternative Sectoral Strategies

The achievement of alternative development in Africa must also grapple with alternative strategies of production and resource management in the major sectors of the economy. The outlines of this rethinking and re-orientation can be indicated briefly for such key sectors as agriculture, industry, technology, etc.

Agriculture and rural development

With the agreed objectives of striving for regional food self-sufficiency in Africa and producing adequate agricultural raw materials for industry and export, the re-orientation of agriculture and rural development is critical. The failed strategies of integrated rural development and 'green revolution' should be discarded. The World Bank's Agricultural Development Projects (ADPs) are also too dependent on capital and other inputs to be sustainable. All these failed agricultural strategies have a common flaw: commodity fetishism. They see the central problem as the production of 'things': food and raw materials. They do not probe enough to explore why these 'things' are not produced.

The necessary re-thinking must situate the agricultural and rural development problem around people, in line with the overall human-centred approach to development. The appalling condition of rural people in most countries is the greatest constraint on agricultural and rural development. This human-centred approach to the understanding of the agrarian crisis also sheds light on why Africa remains the only region in the world that has not yet produced an agrarian revolution. The primitive accumulation of capital that dominates agriculture and rural life is anchored to mass alienation and excessive exploitation, rural powerlessness and unacceptable living conditions. So, first and foremost, rural people must be empowered to participate effectively in decisions over resource allocation to rural areas and agriculture, and in the distribution of their products. This community empowerment will ensure that land, credit, tractors, extension workers, etc. meant for peasants are not cornered by urban absentee landlords, retired grandee bureaucrats, generals and rural kulaks. Better prices can then be obtained as the incentive for increased agricultural production.

Next, the rural areas that harbour the majority of the national population must be made liveable. This requires large investment in all-season feeder roads, trucks and buses (even railways), health clinics, treated water, schools, etc. This will guarantee life to rural dwellers, stem rural-urban migration and encourage 'back to the land' moves among the urban unemployed.

The organization of agricultural production must also change from the current predominant system of small peasant holdings that cannot support the cost of investment in modern techno-logical inputs. Cooperative farming and other rural cooperatives for marketing, pastoralism and women should become predomi-nant. These cooperatives can then be supplemented with state farms where they can be managed efficiently, and with peasant holdings. Land reform should ensure adequate access to land, especially for disadvantaged peasants and women.

It is on this political and social base that modern technology should be applied. This should involve the local manufacturing of tractors, trucks and buses as well as fertilizers and other insecticides. Agro-service centres with adequate numbers of extension workers should make these facilities available to peasants. Rural bank branches and agricultural credit should be mandatory; banks for small-scale enterprises of the cottage industry variety should also be encouraged. In all cases, peasants should control or participate actively in these schemes.

Re-orientation of industrialization

Import substitution industrialization in Africa has been dominated by multinational corporations (mncs) and resulted in industries highly dependent on imports: mere assembly plants, mostly consumer-good enterprises with very low value added. Their heavy reliance on foreign exchange for imported inputs forces these industries to shut down or operate at very low capacity utilization during shortages of foreign exchange. The failure of this import-substitution industrialization strategy with its textile-first approach, emphasizing consumer-good manufacturing and neglecting capital-good production, thus dictates the need for an alternative industrialization strategy.

The de-industrialization strategy of the IMF and World Bank's SAP is equally untenable. By striving for effective leverage over the industrial policy of debtor countries, SAP insists falsely that African countries should concentrate on the export promotion of raw materials and de-emphasize manufacturing because these countries are said to have comparative advantage only in the production of primary products. But this is a facile and imperialist strategy for arresting the industrialization of African countries in order to ensure the cheap supply of raw materials to the advanced countries and prevent Third World industries from competing with the industrial exports of the imperialist countries. This makes an alternative industrialization strategy all the more imperative in Africa.

The *alternative industrial strategy* must be basically inward-looking and self-reliant, both nationally and collectively. It should strive primarily to satisfy domestic demand for manufactured products and be based mainly on local resources. Hence it is often styled the 'domestic demand and local resource' industrial strategy. Its starting point is an assessment of the domestic demand for critical manufactured goods like processed food, drugs, chemicals (e.g., for water treatment), textiles, shoes, vehicles and educational materials among consumer goods; then intermediate products like cement, roofing sheets, paint, insecticides, fertilizers, tractors and steel for agriculture, construction and industry; and basic capital goods like machine tools, petro-chemicals, machinery and transport equipment, etc. These intermediate and capital goods may be too expensive for small African countries to manufacture locally and so they can be produced jointly within cooperative schemes on a sub-regional basis.

Local resources of manpower, capital and raw materials under local sourcing should provide the dominant inputs for the manufacturing of these critical products. In this way, the heavy outlay on imported raw materials can be saved. Mncs typically resist local inputs as inferior and unsatisfactory. Such mncs should be shown the way out of Africa. Thus local sorghum, millet and maize can be used for bread and beer; cassava can be used for starch, clay brick can be substituted for cement, etc. African experts should be mobilized to identify different possible uses for local raw materials and the inventory should be publicized to the business community, researchers and others. In this way manufacturing based on local resources such as agro-allied industries and petroleum-based manufacturing can provide a major catalyst for local manufacturing. Forward and backward integration or linkages can then be developed to expand local industries.

Small-scale enterprises should also receive special emphasis in this alternative strategy. Thus in South-East Asia many of the successful manufacturing enterprises are operated in garages and backyards of family homes. India has a Small-Scale Industry Research Institute that identifies and produces feasibility studies for small enterprises as well as designing simple machines and tools for them. Africa needs similar small-scale enterprise corporations, research institutes and banks that focus on the requirements of cottage industries. These are labour-intensive and can be effective against unemployment, and their artisan technology offers an excellent opportunity for the democratization of technology.

Alternative technology policy

Technology transfer has been a veritable imperialist myth for denying Africa access to technology. Behind the myth lies the reality that technology is not typically transferred; it is adapted, developed indigenously or simply stolen as the advanced countries have been doing for ages. Africa must join this race. The system of industrial property rights — of patents, trademarks, copyrights, etc. — dominated by mncs will not permit free trade in technology. Hence the need to develop indigenous artisan technology and blend it with any additional modern technology that has to be imported and adapted to local needs.

The development of indigenous technology requires two parallel strategies. One is massive science and technology education to be backed with adequate production of books and science equipment as well as serious research funding with the research to be linked to direct producers in different sectors. The other starts with the inventory of local artisan technologies, then develops and modifies them before their wide dissemination. These indigenous efforts can then be supplemented with the import of some specific technologies. For this, a technological data bank on national and collective bases should be developed to store information on types, sources, terms, etc. of different technologies. These imported technologies should be de-mystified by dismantling and re-assembling them before workers. They should then be adapted to local use. In all cases, suppliers of imported technologies should be required to provide local training in their servicing and to provide spare parts (to be produced locally in due course). Technology contracts for training local staff in the operation of imported technology should also be used. Then the standardization of both indigenous and imported technologies should be required to facilitate their mastery and the indigenous production of spare parts.

Conclusion:
Political Programme for Alternative Development

Who will implement these alternative strategies for African development? The answer is a new coalition of class forces comprising patriotic politicians and professionals that must be pressurized by the broad masses of workers, peasants, women, students and progressive intellectuals.

These are the social forces of *Africa's new nationalist movement* — a broad nationalist and democractic front, alliance or syndicate. Africa now faces a *new colonialism* under the Structural Adjustment Programme (SAP) or the Economic Recovery Programme (ERP) and it must respond by recreating the broad nationalist movement on a democratic platform. Its major slogan is Alternative Development, Democracy and Accountability.

The logic of history leaves Africa with little choice. Between the rapid deterioration of the African crisis and the growing involuntary delinking of the continent under the combined pressures of debt crisis, SAP and emerging economic blocs, Africa must rise to the challenge. The current East-West detente, Eastern bloc reforms and competing regional blocs in the West has created a state of flux in the leadership of world imperialism since the October crash of 1987. Africa must exploit the opportunities by charting an alternative normative future and strategic development option.

NOTES

1 See United Nations, *International Development Strategy for the Third UN Development Decade* (New York, 1981).
2 This is a revised version of *ECA and Africa's Development, 1983–2008: a Preliminary Perspective Study* (Addis Ababa, April 1983) which is to be revised every five years.

3 *Revised Perspectives*, Part III, pp. 91—126.
4 See *Revised Perspectives*, Part IV, Section II, pp. 131—202.
5 ECA, *The Khartoum Declaration* (Addis Ababa, 1988).

BIBLIOGRAPHY

Adebayo Adedeji and Timothy Shaw (eds), *Economic Crisis in Africa — African Perspectives in Development Problems and Potentials* (Colerado, 1985).
Adebayo Adedeji, *Towards a Dynamic African Economy* (London, 1989).
Bade Onimode, *A Political Economy of the African Crisis* (London, IFAA/Zed Books, 1988).
Bade Onimode (ed.), *The IMF, the World Bank and the African Debt. Vol. I The Economic Impact, Vol. II The Social and Political Impact* (London, IFAA/Zed Books, 1989).
ECA, *The African Alternative to Adjustment: Programmes for Socio-Economic Recovery and Transformation* (AAF—SAP) (Addis Ababa, 1989).
ECA, *Beyond Recovery — ECA's Revised Perspectives of Africa's Development, 1990—2008* (Addis Ababa, 1989).
Robert Eringer, *The Global Manipulators* (Bristol, Pentacle Books, 1981).
Susan George, *A Fate Worse than Debt* (Penguin, 1988).
R. T. Taylor, *Hot Money and the Politics of Debt* (London, 1988).
UN, *International Development Strategy for the Third United Nations Development Decade* (New York, 1981).
World Bank, *Sub-Saharan Africa: From Crisis to Sustainable Growth — A Long-term Perspective Study* (Washington, 1989).

PART ONE
Keynote Speakers

African Alternatives to World Bank and IMF Programmes

Bade Onimode

I am wearing two caps in this conference. We invited the ECA, the Economic Commission for Africa, to come, but since I was already going to obtain permission from them to attend this conference, they decided that I should represent them. So I am here as a representative of the ECA as well as in my capacity as a member of IFAA.

In introducing the 'African Alternative Framework to Structural Adjustment Programmes for Socio-Economic Recovery and Transformation' (AAF–SAP), I will first put into perspective the whole document and what it tries to do. Since its launch in London in June–July 1989 it has given rise to a very lively debate and, I'm afraid, to some distortions in some quarters, which I will address. In the second part of this presentation I will run through the six chapters. Finally, I'll look at the implications of the document for this conference and for our work.

Background

It is important to say three things right away. First, that the ECA did not just wake up one day and decide to write this document. It is fundamentally an OAU document. I am saying this because the IMF and the World Bank feel that AAF–SAP is a confrontational document, and have been distorting its nature by suggesting that the ECA wants to play a negative role in Africa by producing such a document, to oppose them. That is not the case.

The origins of this document lie in the performance of structural adjustment programmes (SAPs) or economic recovery programmes (ERPs). In some African countries it is called SAP, in others ERP, but essentially it is the same programme. About 33 African countries are implementing this programme, and others are in various stages of negotiations. In most of these countries the result has been disaster.

When African governments and organizations like ours confronted the IMF and the World Bank about the poor performance of SAPs/ERPs the standard response, before June 1989, was always 'What alternative do you have?' So African governments approached the ECA to produce an alternative which they could use in negotiations with the IMF and the World Bank. When the document was produced, it was adopted by African ministers of planning, and then by African finance ministers, at conferences in Lilongwe and in Addis Ababa, and finally adopted by the OAU this year before it was launched. After its launch, the General Assembly of the UN also adopted it on 17 November 1989, as a basis for recovery and transformation in Africa. The vote was 137 for and only one, the United States of America, against. There were no abstentions. So we are talking about a document that has been adopted by the OAU and the UN General Assembly.

The second point is that this alternative is not a programme that is already on the ground. Again the World Bank and the IMF are very fond of saying, 'You don't like SAP, but your own programme is not on the ground.' True, but this document provides a framework, a theoretical basis for designing programmes of recovery and transformation. In other words, on the basis of what is set out here, Tanzania can decide with the collaboration of the IMF/World Bank to design a specific programme for itself, one that does not have to be the same as a programme designed by Uganda. Just as a plan for a room can have all sorts of dimensions, it is possible to construct different programmes that are specific to the different countries on the basis of this plan. The concrete work of elaborating country-specific programmes has yet to be done. So it is neither correct nor logical to accuse this plan of being neither practicable nor operational. It has to be accepted as a basis for negotiation before it can be translated into concrete programmes on the basis of the special circumstances of each country.

The third point we should make, especially in a socialist country like Tanzania, and a progressive conference like this, is that this is not an ideological document in the narrow sense. It is not saying that we should go socialist or we should go capitalist. What it attempts to do is to generate an African nationalist response to what many of us see as the colonial situation in Africa. It is a broad attempt to get a united African front to confront the disastrous policies of the IMF and the World Bank. It will not say that you should nationalize all multinational corporations, that you should socialize all enterprises, although you will find that there are references to the need to have a virile public sector. You will not find in this document a commitment to liberal capitalism either, saying 'Only private enterprise can work in any country'. One reason for this, which you will readily appreciate if you are familiar with the politics of the OAU, is that if you were to produce such a narrow ideological document it would be difficult to get the OAU to adopt it. This is a consensus document, it is up to the individual countries to put their ideological complexion on it.

The intention of this document is that groups like ours and individual African countries can hold it up and say, 'Here is a holistic alternative basis for designing country-specific programmes to replace the existing SAPs. It is a document with which we can do political work, as well as a technical document, although it is an imperfect one. Increasingly, we have to distinguish between technical and political documents. At the end of this year the United Nations will be completing its third UN development decade. UN representatives have confessed that the strategy for the third decade has failed. One major reason for its failure is that it has been restricted to governments and official circles; in other words, it has been essentially a technical and bureaucratic document. I doubt if even ten of us at this conference have seen the document for that development decade. That is why the UN is promising that the document for the fourth UN decade, the 1990s, will be a political document, freely available to people like us and to people in all countries. In that sense the AAF–SAP is also intended to be a political document, to be made widely available and openly debated.

It is imperfect in one respect: it is a bit turgid for non-professional economists. It will therefore go through a second stage in which it will be simplified to a document of 30–50 pages in straightforward English, French and Arabic, accessible to people who at most have secondary school education. That second level is necessary before it can become a fully political document.

Summary of Chapters

Chapter One tries to explain the structure of the African political economy. Many of the policies and programmes on the ground in African countries today are wrong because they are based on a poor understanding of the character of African economies, of the African state and of African society. The chapter deals with the main features of these African economies, in particular to emphasize such features as the excessive external dependence of our countries which constrains our societies. We consume mostly what we don't produce, and produce mostly what we don't consume. There is also extensive 'disarticulation' — major structural deformities and distortions which make different sectors of our economies go in different directions instead of being integrated. As a result we have extensive experience of anti-rural policies that neglect the majority of our people. We have extreme inequalities in social relations: in distribution of wealth, power and social opportunities. Class contradictions have been sharpening in many societies, and within that context we find African societies to be mainly relegated to the production of primary produce in the world economy. That is the kind of situation we want to correct. All of those features of African economies define underdevelopment — which is a lack of adequate productive capacity coupled with external domination and exploitation — as the main problem that African societies have to solve. When we look at the African crisis, especially as manifested in the depression in the 1980s, with debt crises, refugees and so on, one dominant feature is its structural and long-term nature.

World Bank and IMF people tend to look at our problems in purely financial terms. They used to call our crises 'a lack of liquidity' — we don't have enough cash — and these days they call them 'insolvency'. These are ugly words. They are not mine, they are the words of our oppressors. What these people are saying is that our crisis is essentially a crisis of money, especially foreign money. We insist that although we do have these financial problems, they are only reflections, manifestations of production, consumption and distribution, and of power and external relations.

Chapter Two identifies the major development objectives of African economies, which were first spelled out in the Lagos Plan of Action for the Economic Development of Africa 1980—2000. When it was launched in 1980, the World Bank commissioned the Page Report, otherwise called *Towards Accelerated Development in Sub-Saharan Africa*. Whereas the Lagos Plan of Action argued that African countries should come closer together and be inward-looking in their development, the World Bank's report asked for greater external dependence, for 'outward orientation' in our development programmes.

When AAF—SAP was produced, again the World Bank came out with a counter-programme, launched in November 1989 — *Sub-Saharan Africa: from Crisis to Sustainable Development. A long-term perspective study*. Every time African countries and the OAU bring out a document on how we want to develop Africa, the IMF and the World Bank bring out a counter-document.

The main objectives of African economies, as contained in the Lagos Plan of Action, are:

1 Food self-sufficiency on a regional basis

I emphasize regional, because in debates with the IMF and World Bank they think that we want food self-sufficiency country by country, and that's not true. On a scale where ideal self-sufficiency is 100, Africa now stands at around 60–70 per cent, so we are far from ideal.

Some people think that we should ask for 'food security'. The difference between food security and food self-sufficiency is this: food security can be guaranteed through food aid from the advanced countries. We don't have to be told what is wrong with that. As the US did to India, they can decide to give you food today, then tomorrow they can refuse. This is why we are stressing food self-sufficiency on a regional basis, under our own control, as the number one objective.

2 The reduction of general poverty

This translates into satisfying basic, critical needs. In addition to food, these are water, shelter, clothing, education, health, transport, electricity and so on. But if you remove hunger, you remove most of the poverty.

3 The achievement of sustainable development and growth

It is important to emphasize sustainability because it is possible, as the World Bank has reported, to have 5 or 10 per cent growth in one year, and the following year to have zero or negative growth. We want to be sure that production and development can be maintained over time. We want to do all this within a strategy of national and collective self-reliance which would reduce the external dependence of African countries.

Essentially those are the dominant objectives.

When we argue with the IMF and World Bank that their SAPs have failed, they ask: how do you evaluate whether programmes are succeeding or not? The easiest way to do so is to assess them on their own so-called 'performance criteria'. Now, those objectives are not the same as the objectives of the African countries. We must emphasize that.

Chapter three evaluates the performance of the IMF and World Bank stabilization and structural adjustment programmes in different countries. In the process it rejects the February 1989 report of the World Bank and the United Nations Development Programme (UNDP), *Adjustment and Growth in African Countries in the 1980s*. The report is a gross distortion of reality. IFAA was so incensed when it came out that we got in touch with the BBC and entered into a debate with the World Bank. Oxfam joined us in rejecting the report, which claimed that African countries have been growing in the 1980s and that adjustment programmes have been succeeding. I won't waste your time over what is wrong with that claim. If it is true, then why are we here, and why are we saying what we have been saying? We have a separate publication entitled *Statistics and Policies* which gives detailed figures about what is wrong with the position of the World Bank and the UNDP, and therefore of the IMF, on the performance of those programmes. It is very clear that the programmes have failed. Most African people know that as a fact of life. We need an alternative.

We say that the programmes have failed on two grounds. First, on the performance criteria which the present SAPs have laid down for themselves: improvement of the balance of payments, increasing exports, control of inflation and achievement of realistic exchange rates. On the basis of these objectives, which are largely financial, we can go to individual countries and collect figures to see whether those objectives have been satisfied. When you do so, you find that the programmes have failed. The balance of payments position of most African countries has been getting worse. Their exports, especially export revenues, have not been improving. The level of inflation in those countries has not been falling; it has been increasing. The exchange rates in those countries have not been balanced. The real effective rate of exchange, the true measure of performance in terms of devaluation, is supposed to be 100, if these programmes have been working. For most African countries, that real effective exchange rate is now around 20; our national currencies have been destroyed by devaluation and the SAPs. Even on the basis of their own objectives and criteria these programmes have failed.

Second, even if these programmes had succeeded in meeting their own performance targets, we would still consider them as having failed, because they have not satisfied the objectives that African countries have set for themselves. These programmes have not achieved food self-sufficiency for African countries, nor satisfied the critical needs of the majority of African people, and therefore they have not been alleviating poverty. These programmes have achieved neither sustainable growth for African countries, nor self-reliance, either nationally or collectively.

Chapter Four describes the general framework for 'alternative adjustment' in three parts. The first part considers the level of production: food, manufacturing and so forth. The most important economic problem is to increase production in agriculture, in industry, in construction, in services and so on.

The second part considers distribution of what is produced, the distribution of income: what should workers get, what should those who own land get as rent, what should those who save money get as interest? What should the rural population get, what should the urban population get?

The third part considers the kind of policies one must have in order to achieve the production and distribution desired. What policies for money, taxes, government spending and so on, and therefore for the control of foreign trade, should we have? These are the three main pegs of the framework.

We are now building technical econometric models, of the sort the IMF and World Bank people like to play with. They are fond of saying, 'Ah, you see, we have an econometric model!' Well, we have looked at their model and it is useless! Many African professional economists are now consultants to the IMF/World Bank — I would be surprised if this university does not have some of them — and we want to send a message to them. We have thrown down the same challenge to the IMF and World Bank: to show us, through any kind of technical, economic manipulation, that the three policies discussed below can work, anywhere in Africa.

First, *devaluation of currency*. Tanzania devalued by about 70 per cent recently; it doesn't work, and it has never worked. Altogether, since these programmes started in this country, the Tanzanian shilling has been devalued by over 500 per cent. There is no way you can devalue to that extent and get good results. The Nigerian naira has been devalued by over 600 per cent, and the result is disaster. We challenge these bourgeois economists and their IMF and World Bank bosses to show how devaluation on that scale can work in Africa. If they think they can prove it, we know we can disprove it: a technical, professional challenge.

Second, show us how the *high interest rates* which they have been recommending, from 10—12 per cent to about 30 per cent — can increase savings and therefore increase the inflow of capital as they predict. They tell us we must produce what they call 'positive, real rates of interest', that is, the difference between the money rate of interest and the rate of increase of prices. They say that we should do so because we must increase savings. That theory of savings is outdated by more than one hundred years. We know today that savings do not depend on the rate of interest; they depend on the level of income. Again, we challenge these economists to show us models where similar increases in interest rates have increased savings. Our own studies have shown that wherever rates of interest have increased so much, savings have fallen.

Third, show us countries where the *liberalization of trade* can be used as a basis for improving the balances in the economy — because everywhere they go they say we must remove all controls on foreign trade.

Our challenges are serious. These people have been telling our governments that if they don't do so and so, the economy will not improve. Country after country has been following these policies and their economies have been getting worse and worse. We can show that they cannot work and that they are not meant to work.

Chapter Five proposes alternative policies. It is important, first, to emphasize one point. The IMF and World Bank policies and programmes have dictated that you must stabilize and adjust first; after that, you can try to resume growth. We don't accept that. There is a conceptual error in that formulation. When you say 'first, stabilize', you assume — wrongly — that before the present crisis our economies had balance or equilibrium. That is not true. All students of development economics know that when you have an underdeveloped country you have a system of imbalance, of disequilibrium.

It is useless trying to say that you want to adjust back to balance, which was not there in the first place, before you can move forward. Our countries' economies, since the days of the slave trade and right through the colonial era, have never been in equilibrium. The same is true of all Third World countries. What we need is not a set of policies that will bring about balance, but a set of policies that will manage the imbalance, reduce its extent. We will not achieve stabilization or adjustment as long as we are underdeveloped countries. The real task is to achieve development and structural transformation; to eliminate mass poverty. If you can do that, you will remove the causes of imbalance. What we need is simultaneous growth with adjustment; development and stabilization must be pursued together, at the same time.

The IMF and the World Bank are now protesting, 'Oh, we are

not saying that you should not grow'. But they used to say so. Now, under pressure, they are changing their tune. Even as they agree with us that we should try to achieve balance with growth, they have still not translated that agreement into concrete policies on the ground.

There is no way in which you can use the original IMF model to bring about growth. When we discussed this with the IMF recently they said they have changed that model for another, so that they can bring about growth. We are saying we want to see it. Our alternative demands development and growth along with adjustment and stabilization. We do not want to wait to finish adjustment before we can grow. We want to do the two together, and Chapter Five sets out six major alternative policies.

1 Exchange rates

Here we have two arguments. The first is that massive devaluation has failed. It cannot work and we should stop it. What it does is to destroy the currencies of African countries. Instead, we should allow currencies to depreciate. Second, in many of our countries the IMF and World Bank have been asking us to have 'currency auctions' as they did in Zambia, in Ghana, in Nigeria. They are still doing it in Nigeria. Every day or week you bring out so many dollars and ask people how much they will pay for each dollar in local currency. That is a system of flexible exchange rates; you allow the rate to go up and down. The general direction is therefore to make your currency convertible. That is not good for small countries in world trade. What we need instead is a system of fixed exchange rates which can be reviewed from time to time. For example, Tanzania could say 'We want to stop this devaluation. We are going to fix the rate of exchange between the shilling and the US dollar at about 30 to the dollar.' You fix it there, and you leave it for about three to six months. You look at the result, and then you can jack it up or bring it down. A crawling peg, they call it. By the way, when it achieves monetary union in 1992, Europe is planning to use this fixed exchange rate — in the Exchange Rate Mechanism of the European Monetary System — which the IMF and World Bank has been saying is no good for our countries.

In addition, we are saying that African countries should be free, on a temporary basis, to have more than one rate of exchange. We will divide our demand for foreign goods and services into two: essential imports — like drugs, chemicals, food and so on — will have a higher exchange rate. Tanzanians can decide, for example, if an importer wants to buy medicines, to give him dollars at the rate of 30 shillings to $1. Then for other, non-essential imports they can ask up to 50 or 100 shillings for $1. Especially if you want dollars. If you import shoes, shirts, whisky, Mercedes-Benz, these useless things that we don't need, you should pay more. Yes, it is true that there may be corruption. They tell us, 'Your bureaucrats are corrupt, and if you do that the result will be bad.' The question is, since even with the present system there is corruption, who gets the benefit of the corruption? The past system of controls used to benefit the corrupt civil servants. The present system, with market forces, is now benefiting the bankers. In any case, there is nothing that says we cannot reduce the level of corruption in our countries. At least as a temporary measure, we should have multiple exchange rates and fix them so that we can regulate.

If you look at a country like Ethiopia, one reason why they seem to do better than many other African countries, in spite of their war, is that exchange rates between the Ethiopian currency and the dollar have been fixed for about ten years, at about 2.02 *birr* to $1. When I was on sabbatical in Ethiopia during 1981—82, it was the same rate as it is today. That is what we need, so that currencies do not dance up and down like a yo-yo.

The IMF and World Bank say our currencies are over-valued; that we are giving too few Tanzanian shillings for the dollar. When Tanzania was giving 20 shillings to the dollar, it was 'overvalued'. Now that it is around 200 shillings to the dollar, we are asking the Americans to pay half a cent instead of five cents for one Tanzanian shilling. How far down do we have to go? In Nigeria now the official rate is about 7.5 *naira* to the US dollar. As a result, at a five-star Nigerian hotel an American can pay about forty dollars for a suite or a double room. If you were to go to the West holding forty dollars, you wouldn't get a single bed in a cheap hotel. Through this devaluation we are subsidizing the rich countries: they are now getting our raw materials almost free. That is one of the objectives of their structural adjustment, and it is why we say it a fraudulent programme of re-colonization.

2 Interest rates

We are suggesting that the rate of interest should be lowered in most African countries. In particular, African governments should be able to determine the priority areas in which they want to spend their money. It is not only the forces of demand and supply that should determine who gets bank loans. In addition, governments should be able to say, 'We have priority programmes like agriculture, health, education, and basic industries. For those industries, we should give guidelines to allocate credit.'

3 Subsidies

Just as the US and EEC are giving subsidies to their agriculture, African countries should be allowed to give selective subsidies for production. It is true that subsidies have been abused in the past, but to withdraw all of them is not the solution.

4 Trade liberalization

Even the US and EEC are quarrelling with Japan and the other

South-East Asian countries because these Asian countries are 'dumping' their exports. The US and the EEC are now producing anti-dumping laws against exports from South-East Asia. Yet at the same time they are telling African countries to open up their imports. If the US and EEC need anti-dumping laws to protect themselves against smaller competitors, how much more control do African countries need against imperialist countries? We don't accept import liberalization, because we need more control.

5 Privatization

It is clear that the IMF and World Bank are talking about privatization as part of a doctrinaire, dogmatic programme. They want to impose liberal capitalism on all African countries. Here there is a theory of collective guilt. When they announced these measures, they said, 'Public enterprises have failed in all countries.' They say governments are corrupt in all countries. How can that be? How can all governments be corrupt and everything be bad? For example, Ethiopian Airlines is one of the best airlines in the world, by any standard. Yet this is a public enterprise. Many public enterprises in African countries are making profits, and yet they are being privatized. What is there that says governments should not make profits? Privatization should not be a dogmatic thing. In areas where government can do well, let the government do it. In areas where private enterprise can do well, maybe let them do it. On the basis of ideological choice, each country should decide what to do, but there should not be a dogmatic programme selling public enterprise at any cost. One other possibility apart from privatization is commercialization, in which you establish rules according to which public enterprises should operate.

6 Export promotion

There should not be general export promotion; it should be

selective, because if you make it general you run into a problem. For example, last year we heard that the Ivory Coast doubled its exports of cocoa, yet its total export revenue fell by 50 per cent. Why? Because the demand for cocoa has been falling, as is the demand for exports of all African countries. When the foreign demand for exports is falling, if you say you must increase exports at any cost, you are asking for disaster. We have calculated that African countries have lost, from about 1980 to the present, export earnings that amount to even more than our total foreign debt. The United States, since the time of Reagan, has been increasing restrictions on imports from our countries. Technical progress has reduced demand for exports by 30 per cent through synthetic substitutes.

Chapter Six talks about how to implement AAF–SAP. The basic recommendation is that there should be democratization: popular participation by groups such as ours.

Policy Implications

Finally, what are the policy implications of this document? This has to be a political document: it can only be implemented through pressure by groups like ours and other people in African countries. We must insist that the IMF should negotiate with African countries on the basis of AAF–SAP so that this document can be used for designing alternative programmes for recovery and transformation in Africa.

REPLIES TO QUESTIONS FROM THE FLOOR

Why are we using World Bank statistics?
To evaluate the World Bank's programmes we should proceed in two stages. First, we should use their own figures, their own language, to see whether what they have set out to do has been

done. So we use their own figures, to show them that even what they have said they would do, they have not done. Then we go a step further, to say even if the figures show that they have done what they set out to do, that does not solve our problems. What we show in Chapter Three is that they have manipulated the figures.

In his letter of resignation, Mr Budhoo of the IMF accused the organization of systematically manipulating figures in Third World countries in order to produce bogus results. That allegation was probed by an international group of experts and was found to be correct. Mr Budhoo has now proceeded to expand the letter — which was about fifty pages long — into a book called *Dear Mr Kamdessus* (the managing director of the IMF), which is to be published by Zed Books.

A book by Percy Mistry, who has resigned from the World Bank, is also highly critical. It is based on a lecture given in London on World Bank policies and has been produced by IFAA.

Is there an alternative to the IMF?
Yes, there is an alternative to the IMF. But the IMF belongs to us. Africa is part of this planet, and nobody is going to will us away. Our money is in it, even though we are in debt. We are not the only ones in debt: the US is the greatest debtor country in the world, and is not under SAPs.

There is no question of the IMF setting arbitrary conditions for our participation in it. Whether they like it or not we are going to inherit the earth with them, and therefore the institutions created for the world concern all of us equally.

In 1942, Britain was indebted to the US. At that point the debt service of Britain was pegged at 2 per cent. Today African countries are being made to pay 40 per cent. During the monetary disorders of the 1970s in Europe what was the discipline of the IMF? It gave a loan of 2 billion dollars to the Boers in South Africa. What was the conditionality attached to it? It is on these grounds that we reject their conditions. We are going to continue to take their money. It is part of our money. It belongs to the world. In Europe they tell us that they would not accept 10 per cent of these bogus conditions that the IMF and the others impose on us.

In fairness to these institutions, they tell us they have talked to our governments, who say they agree, when they send documents to us they are to be debated. In many cases when these documents arrive in our countries, they are put under lock and key and marked *Secret*. Part of the problem is internal. That doesn't mean that you and I accepted SAP. We were not consulted. Even though the IMF and World Bank are screaming 'democratization' in Europe, when they come to our countries they encourage dictatorship. When they come to sign these agreements they talk to one or two people in our ministries, one or two ministers, then they sign. They know that in their countries that is not how to proceed. But they endorse it here. They know that most of the loans they give to our countries are stolen and kept in secret bank accounts in Europe and North America. They connive with our leaders to loot our countries. These are the things we say must stop. This document is very clear. There is corruption in Africa: there is nothing to hide. But that corruption cannot be perpetuated. Some of the leaders in our countries are being kept in power by those who back the IMF and World Bank. When Zambia rejected the SAP in May 1987, and laid down its own national programme, the IMF and the World Bank rejected it until December last year. So it is not internal problems alone. The total budget of many African countries is less than the assets of one multi-national corporation. In addition, the creditor countries have ganged up: look at the Club of Paris, Club of London, Group of Seven.... Yet when African countries want to come together, the IMF and World Bank throw up their hands in horror and say, 'Look!' Groups like our own have to come into the debate, to say that we don't accept these conditions. In the past the IMF and the World Bank used to insist on stabilization alone: with sufficient pressure now they are saying 'stabilization with growth'. We must sustain that pressure. They must give more.

Do we accept the need for industrialization?
Yes, we accept it. This document does not yet have enough detailed strategies for industry, for agriculture and so on, but when the individual country programmes are being designed, these detailed strategies will be spelled out. This is why at this conference we are going to evolve strategies apertaining to the different sectors: that will be the next stage.

Labour and Structural Adjustment Programmes

Hassan Sunmunu

I would like to express my gratitude to the director and members of the council of IFAA for the invitation extended to me and other leaders of the Organization of African Trade Union Unity (OATUU) to attend this conference. I was equally privileged to attend the institute's conference on the impact of the IMF and the World Bank on the peoples of Africa, which took place in London in September 1987. The contribution to the debate on the impact of IMF and World Bank policies in Africa at the IFAA London conference opened the way to the critical examination of the policies of these two financial organizations. It is my hope that the present conference will likewise show the way to alternative strategies for Africa's development.

Before we consider new strategies for development in Africa we should first review the present strategies and then decide whether there is a need to continue with them or change them. As we all know, at least 33 African countries have been forced to adopt the IMF programme for structural adjustment. As a result of heavy external debt and balance of payment difficulties, Africa is estimated to owe US$230 billion at the end of 1989. The main causes of Africa's debt problems can be summarized as follows:

1   The narrow range of export commodities, since most African countries rely on one or two main exports, be they agricultural or mineral.

2   Unstable and low commodity prices. For example, Africa lost

an estimated US$19 billion in export earnings between 1985 and 1986.

3   Unfair terms of trade.

4   Neglect of agriculture and rural areas.

5   Sharp practices by multinational corporations through transfer pricing.

6   Corruption in high and low places.

Interest Payments and IMF Conditionalities

Of all the external loans taken by African countries, the most worrisome were the ones from international banks. These had the highest interest rates and in most cases no fixed interest rates. The interest was tied to the prevailing interest rates of the countries of the creditor banks. For example, it was 1 per cent above LIBOR (London Interbank Official Rate) for banks of the London Club. Any time the British Chancellor of the Exchequer raises the interest rates, it automatically increases the debts of debtor countries to the London Club members. That is how African and other Third World debts increase by leaps and bounds in spite of the fact that the principal and interest, if calculated at 6 per cent, have been paid at least twice over.

The main features of the IMF conditionalities implemented under the current structural adjustment programmes are:

1   Massive devaluation of the national currency.

2   Massive reduction in number of public sector employees: between 30 and 40 per cent retrenchment.

3   Trade liberalization.

4   Privatization of public sector companies.

5   Supervision and approval of all fiscal, budgetary and development plans and policies, including the central banks, by the IMF.

Consequences of the SAPs

Now let us examine the consequences of these IMF and World Bank structural adjustment programmes for the economies of African countries and the lives of the African people. The IMF, to those of us in trade union circles in Africa and throughout the world, is a surgeon from whose operating theatre no patient comes out alive. And it is a bogus doctor who prescribes the same medicine for different ailments. The main argument used to justify the massive devaluation of the national currency is 'market forces', the rule of demand and supply. This is an argument that has no political or economic basis because it does not take into consideration the purchasing power parity of the currency. It should also be remembered that there is no currency in the world whose value is fixed only on the consideration of so-called market forces. The gross undervaluation of African currencies is the factor most responsible for the continuously falling standard of living of our people; the brain drain and the inability of our local industries to compete with foreign industries, leading to progressive de-industrialization of African countries and the loss of millions of jobs.

On trade liberalization, I challenge anybody to show me any country in the world that does not protect its agriculture and industries in one way or another. Is it the European Economic Community or the United States of America, or Japan? Why are the IMF and World Bank people blackmailing poor African and other debtor countries to liberalize their trade? The threat posed by the trade liberalization measures African countries are forced to undertake is the destruction of industries in our country, the loss of millions of jobs and the conversion of our countries into mere markets for the finished goods of the developed countries. This is a situation that is not only unacceptable to African workers and the OATUU, but is also unjust and inequitable. We should all remember the African proverb that says: 'Eating together is not good if some are satisfied and others are still hungry.'

A trade liberalization policy often involves the removal of government subsidies on food, education, health, housing, transport and agriculture, leading to high food prices, malnutrition and hunger, rapid drops in school enrolment, acute shortages of housing and high rents, and inadequate, expensive transportation.

This inhuman policy affects the most vulnerable in the society: the poor, the children and the aged. Is it any wonder, then, that there are an estimated 103 million hungry people in Africa? Where is the development when over 20 per cent of Africa's population is hungry? Because for us development begins from here, from the stomach.

Massive retrenchment in the public sector is justified by the economic rules of the IMF and World Bank on the grounds that the public sectors of the debtor countries are 'too large and unproductive', to quote them. When doctors, engineers, technologists, technicians, teachers and so on are forcibly retrenched, who is going to tap and develop the human and natural resources of Africa for its development? I would like the IMF and World Bank officials to answer this question.

The privatization of public companies, is, to say the least, the process of converting the African commonwealth into common poverty, so that a microscopic minority of Africans — less than 1 per cent — and their foreign backers can be super-rich. Are the majority of African people who are sapped under the present harsh economic conditions and on the 010 or 101 [Mills] formula, capable of buying the 'shares' of the about-to-be-privatized public companies? The ideologues of privatization have been harping on efficiency and profitability as the criteria favouring the privatization of state-owned companies. They should then answer the following questions:

1   Efficiency of capital comes at what social cost?

2   Profitability in what economic and social sense?

Time will not permit me to answer these two questions for the apostles of privatization, but permit me to quote part of the conclusion of the recent OATUU seminar on the role and place of the public sector in development, which was held in Accra, 19—21 September 1989:

> The reason for the existence of any government, no matter what its character, should be the satisfaction of the basic needs of the people. The needs, such as employment, food, shelter, health, education, water, electricity, transport and communications, are the main criteria for development. The most appropriate agency employed by the government for the achievement of these objectives is the public sector. This sector is therefore the vehicle for development. In order that the public sector may respond to the changing circumstances in every country, it should therefore be preserved, developed, and transformed — not privatized as the IMF/World Bank are insisting and blackmailing our governments to do.

I completely share this view, because the public service is the backbone of any government, be it in developed or developing, capitalist or socialist countries. Because of the low level of industrialization in Africa, the public sector will continue for a long time to come to play a key role in the development of Africa. In our economic and social context in Africa, to destroy the public sector is to destroy the continent. May God forbid that. The supervision and approval by the IMF and World Bank officials of all fiscal, budgetary and development plans and policies is the greatest manifestation of loss of sovereignty by African countries implementing the Structural Adjustment Programmes. One can only say that Africans did not fight the war of independence only to lose, thirty years later, the battle for economic sovereignty. From all the above, and from the data compiled by other UN agencies, like the ECA, UNICEF, ILO and so on, and from the OATUU's own analysis, there is no iota of doubt that the SAPs have woefully failed. They have failed because they have led to vast poverty, high unemployment and underemployment, malnutrition, hunger and death, increasing illiteracy, widening societal inequity and inequality, the violation of human and trade union rights, erosion of the basic rights of the people, leading to worsening conditions of living, violations of the democratic rights of the people, increased spending on arms, violation of the sovereignty of African countries, and mortgaging of the future development, prosperity and happiness of African people. It is on the basis of all this that we maintain that there is no single success story of the IMF/World Bank Structural Adjustment Programmes in Africa.

Honestly, bothers and sisters, it has no success, not even in Ghana. I live in Ghana. I know what happens in Ghana. There's nobody earning any salary, no matter the level, without doing some other work. Nobody who can actually maintain himself today in Ghana on one job. So don't believe what they are telling you. They are lying and they know they are lying.

Alternative Strategies for Development

We move on to strategies for development. (Please forgive me if I have spent a long time diagnosing in some detail the effects of the IMF and World Bank Structural Adjustment Programmes on African countries. Don't doctors say that the correct diagnosis of the disease is half the cure?)

What then is development? Secondly, what should be the objectives of development? And thirdly, who should be the beneficiaries of development? The *Chambers Dictionary* defines development as

> the act or process of developing; state of being developed; a gradual unfolding of growth; evolution, the expression of a function in the form of a series in maths; elaboration of a theme or that part of a movement in which there is a cause [music]; new situations that arise ....

In the context of this conference my own definition of development is 'the satisfaction and continuous improvement of the basic needs of people and the maintenance of the environment'. By basic needs I mean employment, food, shelter (housing), health, education, water, electricity, transport and communications. These are the parameters by which development should be measured. A country that cannot or has not succeeded in satisfying the basic needs of its people cannot be said to be developed.

So we come to the next question. The objectives of development should be as envisaged in the Lagos Plan of Action, that is:

1 the alleviation of mass poverty and the improvement of standards of living of the African people;
2 the satisfaction of the basic needs of the African people;
3 the achievement of the objectives of a national and regional collective self-reliance.

As regards the third question, the entire people of a country or continent should be the beneficiaries of development. In other words, all development should be people-oriented. Any other kind is not development.

Having defined development, its objectives and targets, we can now discuss strategies. The strategies should help in transforming the economy of Africa from a dependent economy into a self-reliant economy. The foundation stones of strategies for development in Africa should be:

1 development of human resources;
2 satisfaction and continuous inprovement of the basic needs of the African peoples;
3 maintenance of a healthy environment;
4 creation and generation of employment;
5 food security and food self-sufficiency;
6 population management;
7 integrated industrialization;
8 development of sports and culture;
9 the integration of African economies;
10 full participation of the people in all aspects of governance.

1 Development of human resources

It is a fact universally acknowledged that investment in human resources is the key to independence in government. A country or continent where a large percentage of the people is illiterate cannot be considered as developed. Africa should therefore embark immediately on a massive literacy programme to eradicate illiteracy from the continent by the year 2000. Governments, employers, trades unions, religious institutions, women and youth organizations, the armed forces, schools, colleges, and universities should be actively involved in this programme. Curricula of primary and secondary schools should emphasize agricultural, technical and technological subjects without neglecting the sociological and cultural aspects of African society. Similarly, polytechnics and universities should lay the same emphasis in their curricula; each of them should have their own teacher training department or faculty. Access to education is a fundamental human right. Therefore, education should not only be free at all levels, but it should also be accessible to all, and relevant to the development needs of the country or continent. Education can conveniently be financed through a system of taxation and the savings that can be made by a 10−20 per cent reduction of arms purchases in each African country.

2 Satisfaction and continuous improvement of basic needs

In order to satisfy the basic needs (as earlier defined) of the African peoples, the political will of African governments and peoples must be harnessed. This is the only way to eliminate mass poverty and increase the welfare of the people. It is well stated in the ECA's AAF−SAP:

> It should be emphasized that the urgency of eliminating mass poverty and increasing the welfare of the African people is rooted not simply in the humanistic or altruistic aspects of development. It is predicated, above all, on the

rational proposition that development has to be engineered and sustained by the people themselves through their full and active participation. Development should not be undertaken on behalf of a people; rather, it should be the organic outcome of a society's value system, its perceptions, its concerns and its endeavours. As such, to achieve and sustain development it is necessary to ensure the education and training, health, well-being, and vitality of the people so that they can participate fully and effectively in the developmental process.

3 Maintenance of a healthy environment

The drought of the Sahel region of Africa in the early 1980s was the first signal of our misuse of the African environment. Bush-burning for agriculture, timber-felling for wood export and firewood for cooking have all led to the desertification of millions of hectares of fertile land all over Africa. It has also led to food shortage and sudden climatic changes including heatwaves and short, insufficient rainfall. The policies so far adopted by African governments have been half-hearted and inadequate. There is therefore the urgent need for African governments and all the continents' social partners to take comprehensive measures to protect the African environment. The following suggestions should be seriously considered:

- The education and encouragement of all citizens to love nature. Each household should plant trees and flowers. All urban and village roads should be lined with trees, not only to provide shelter but also for beauty and for the production of life-giving oxygen.
- Urban and rural dwellers should be encouraged to install cheap and subsidised stoves using either groundnut-shell briquettes — as perfected by Senegal and Gambia for groundnut-producing countries — or gas in oil-producing African countries, or electricity where energy is available and cheap.

- Mass organizations like trade unions, employers' associations, women's, farmers' and youth organizations, Boy Scouts, Girl Guides, youth corps, public and private companies and armed forces should be provided with tree seedlings to plant and maintain on a regular basis in all desert and erosion-prone areas of Africa.
- Systematic planting of early-maturing tree seedlings should by law be made mandatory for all companies engaged in the logging business in Africa.
- There should be strict legal control of the observance of international safety standards.
- Overgrazing by cattle should be avoided.
- There should be selective use of fertilizers to avoid pollution of African rivers.
- Several national game parks should be created, preserved and maintained in every African country. Game poaching should be made a criminal offence.

4 The creation and generation of employment

All government programmes in Africa should have employment creation, generation and training components. The choice of investment and investors should be predicated on the above three components. The public, parastatal and private sectors, the trade unions and employers' organizations, cooperatives and individual citizens should also complement the efforts of African governments in the creation and generation of employment. The all-round development of Africa is, and should be, the responsibility of African governments, organizations and peoples. We have no alternative other than to rely on ourselves. Self-reliance in Africa should not be a mere slogan. It should be an article of faith for all of us. Not less than 10 per cent of the annual budget of African countries should be diverted to productive ventures that generate and create employment.

5 Food security and food self-sufficiency

Now that the bitter lessons have been learned from the lower prices fetched by African agricultural products, due in the case of cocoa and coffee to over-production, it is obvious that African countries should shift the emphasis of agricultural policy to the production of food in order to ensure food security and food self-sufficiency for their countries. Less than 10 per cent of African countries are self-sufficient in food. The majority of them spend millions of dollars on food imports. This money should have been more usefully spent developing the agricultural potential of these countries.

Agricultural policy has been biased against the small farmers who constitute the largest producers of food and cash crops on the continent. In order, therefore, to remedy this sad situation, the following measures should be adopted by African countries:

- Henceforth the small, mostly peasant African farmers should be the centre of all agricultural policies and programmes.
- Agrarian reforms should be introduced where necessary, as in Egypt in 1952 and subsequent years, to allow peasants, including women, to own their farms.
- Peasants and other farmers should be assisted technically through agricultural extension workers, with improved seeds, fertilizers, machines, credit, etc.
- Agricultural cooperatives and marketing should be encouraged, promoted and assisted.
- Silos and other agricultural warehouses should be built and agricultural prices should be subsidized to ensure profitability for farmers and encourage them to produce more cheaply and efficiently.
- Agricultural and rural areas should be improved through the provision of all-season roads, water and electricity supplies, and agricultural and rural industries. A country that does not subsidize its agriculture will never be self-sufficient in food. We have only to consider the examples of the US, still

subsidizing its agriculture, and the EEC, doing likewise through its Common Agricultural Policy (CAP). Yet the World Bank and IMF put pressure on our governments to remove the subsidies on our farmers and on our agriculture. You can see the new colonialism in that aspect.

It is now generally recognized that food is a weapon of war. It is also a weapon of foreign policy. We should, however, not forget the proverb that says 'When hunger is removed from poverty, there is no poverty any more' — an African proverb. Poverty begins in the stomach.

6 Population management

Talking about population reminds me of the Yoruba proverb that goes:

I had wanted to have twenty children like the grass. I also wanted to have thirty children like a river. But instead of having two thousand dirty and lazy children, I would rather have one brilliant and very successful child.

Apart from a very few African countries — less than five, actually — the continent has still to implement effective population policies that will lead to good spacing of children, to a manageable number. In this regard some simple traditional birth control methods, that constitute no health hazards to either the male or the female user, should be identified, developed and adapted for use. Our people have traditional means of birth control but because of modern medicine we have neglected them. I think we should resuscitate them. Massive public education programmes should be mounted to promote population management. Without this, there will be a population explosion in Africa and development will be in serious jeopardy.

7 Integrated industrialization

About 70 per cent of Africa's population is engaged in agriculture.

Agriculture should therefore form the basis of Africa's industrialization. The main objective should, however, be to satisfy the food needs of the continent and then to export both food and agricultural produce in processed and packaged forms. What we are doing now is just exporting raw cocoa, raw coffee and so on. In the case of African countries that have an abundance of mineral resources, like oil, gas, copper, gold, bauxite, tin, diamonds, iron, or coal, etc., their processing should take into consideration the sub-regional and continental markets and needs and the forward and backward linkages. For example, the establishment of a cement factory, even where the materials are locally available, should be linked to the construction industry in the whole sub-region, that is, housing programmes, roads, airports and ports construction, so as to ensure optimum capacity utilization of the factory, which will in turn reduce the cost of production and increase profitability. The cutting and polishing of diamonds will give a higher value-added income to the countries exporting raw and uncut diamonds like Ghana and Sierra Leone. The same could be said of gold. Joint ventures among African governments' local and foreign investors will speed up Africa's industrialization.

8 Development of sports and culture

It is said that a healthy mind resides in a healthy body. The development of all kinds of sports, either for leisure or for competition, should be embarked upon by African countries. Apart from the benefits derived from sports such as good health and recreation, sports bring glory and wealth to individuals and countries. Sports like football, lawn tennis, boxing, golf, basketball, even athletics, have today become flourishing modern industries, not to mention the industries created for their equipment. The Olympic Games have shed their modesty of making athletes content themselves with mere participation. Winning at the Olympics is now the main attraction for parti-cipation. Another aspect of sport is that it can be used as a political weapon. Africa has successfully used sport as a weapon to fight apartheid in racist South Africa. Africa still has a long way to go in sport, in spite of our good performance in athletics, boxing and football. For Africa to be in the first league within the next few years in all sports, the following should be done:

- Build stadia and other sports facilities.
- Train coaches, athletes and other sportsmen and women constantly.
- Encourage the young and the old to participate in sports.
- Produce good but cheap sports equipment on a large scale.
- Organize national, regional, sub-regional, continental and international competitions.
- Develop and promote professionalism in major sports.

CULTURE

The preservation of the best in African culture should be given priority by African countries and peoples. Oral and written history should be preserved and taught in educational institutions throughout the continent. So must African music, folklore and dances. African artists, painters, sculptors, singers, musicians, writers and choreographers should be discovered, encouraged and promoted. African dresses, arts and crafts should be popularized and commercialized in and out of the continent. African languages should be taught at schools in all African countries. Principal African languages like Swahili, Hausa and Arabic should be taught in schools throughout the continent alongside other international languages like English, French and Portuguese. More African films, music, plays etc. should occupy and dominate the screens and airwaves of the television and radio stations in African countries.

9 The integration of African economies

The objective of the integration of African economies should be as stated in the AAF—SAPs of the ECA. That is, regional collective self-reliance. It is increasingly becoming clear that with the European single market of 1992, the trade pact between the USA and Canada, etc., African countries have no alternative for their future survival and development other than intra-African trade and African economic integration. There is evidence of growing trade barriers, in spite of the efforts of UNTAG. The development of Africa and its future prosperity are linked to intra-African trade and economic integration. Otherwise the entire continent will be marginalized and condemned to being a mere raw material provider for the rest of the world. God forbid that.

10 Democracy, human rights, and the full participation of the people in all aspects of governance

These are conditions for development. If people are not involved in the development process, how can they effectively contribute their quota? Governments then become distant and alienated from the people, like the colonial governments in their last years before independence. African countries should not only respect but also uphold and practise the principles enshrined in the United Nations Declaration of Human Rights and the African Charter on Human and People's Rights. A number of African countries have violated these rights. The withdrawal or violation of any of these rights by any African authority is a betrayal of the trust of the African peoples. Democracy and human rights will mean nothing if they are not accompanied by social and economic justice. We should all be, in the truest sense of African culture and tradition, our brother's keeper. God bless Africa.

Church and Society in Africa

Bishop Henry Okullu

I wish to reflect with you on the role of Church and state in the task of development. This is fraught with problems. I have just presided over a major conference on the mission of the Church in Kenya today. Those of you who see Kenyan newspapers must have witnessed the political backlash provoked by one or two resolutions of the Conference. Its near miraculous for me to be here after that gruelling experience.

Another obvious difficulty lies in writing a paper about a large continent like Africa, parts of which I have not visited. To compound the problem there are many Church traditions with social concerns different to those I believe to be derived from biblical faith. I stand here as an East African with an Anglican Church tradition but with deep concern and long ecumenical experience in Africa and beyond.

Let us first try to remember what kind of societies the African political leadership set out to build when we became politically autonomous in the 1960s. According to their stated objectives, nations were to be socialist (African) communities in which persons and their roles in society would not depend on the size of house, or the number of cars, wives and children they had. Human dignity was to be respected and upheld and every person would have the right to be heard and the freedom to participate in the politics of his country. The new nations would respect the homogeneity and cultural heritage of existing communities and base the new national life on them. Independent institutions, trade unions, associations of intellectuals, student movements, women's organizations, the Church and the rest would be strengthened to become pillars of society. The rights of minority and opposition parties would be allowed and protected and, where parties did not exist, free discussion between the rulers and the ruled would prevail.

In achieving these goals and objectives religion or the Church was considered to be an important factor, as is clearly stated in Kenya's Sessional Paper No. 10 on African Socialism.

Another fundamental force in African traditional life was religion which provided a strict moral code for the community. This will be a prominent feature of African socialism.[1]

Many African states are secular, such as Nigeria, Togo, the Ivory Coast, Kenya and Uganda. Mozambique is semi-secular and semi-atheist. Liberia is perhaps the only state in Africa which specifically states in its constitution that it is Christian. In Nigeria, Burundi, Madagascar and Mauritius the state gives some subsidies to the Churches or exempts them from a number of taxes. In Kenya, the Churches are allowed to bring in duty-free vehicles, depending on the mood of the day. In most of these states — even those which declare themselves to be secular — religion plays a major role in society. Kenya, Uganda (except during Amin's bid to Islamize it) and Tanzania are secular states. Many people, including the majority of politicians and civil servants, are members of one religion or another. In Kenya, almost every government function begins with prayer. Former President Nyerere once declared 'Tanzania has no religion': the party had no religion; the government had no religion. But almost all Tanzanians are religious people, and the party and the government guarantees each citizen the right to choose his own religion. Thus these states are secular only in the sense that their constitutions do not specifically state that they are based on Christian principles.

Many political leaders have made clear their positions concerning the relationship between Church and state. President

Moi was reported to have made the following statement when he met the Anglican Bishop at State House in Nairobi in January 1981:

> He urged Churches not to relax their efforts in preaching spiritual matters, adding that preaching the Holy Scriptures helped the Government maintain stability. He called on Churches and all able-bodied in society to help those who could not help themselves. He stressed that religion was not a privilege but a right and said that Churches should regard themselves as part and parcel of Government.[2]

Mwai Kibaki, then Kenya's Vice-President, has been the most outspoken leader in Kenya on the relation between Church and state:

> Politics and religion are inseparable. To suggest that politics should be left to the politicians and religion to the clergy, is a terrible intellectual arrogance.... This way tends to suggest that through some mysterious magical process, some politicians have become specially qualified to be the only ones to pronounce on political issues.[3]

Mwai Kibaki believes that it is through the involvement of Church leaders in public affairs that Africa can retain its soul. Various politicians and civil servants had on numerous occasions asserted that the Church's responsibility was to pray for the government and to help the people to keep the peace. They had warned that the government could remove the government-given freedom of worship. This is a God-given right which the government has the obligation to protect in the same way it protects other rights.

Before 1986, there had never been any open conflict between Church and state in Kenya. Kenyatta could not have wanted that kind of confrontation and the leadership of the National Christian Council of Kenya (NCCK) was considered to be very close to Kenyatta. Secondly, as control of the government machinery was to a large extent in the hands of the Kikuyus, the predominantly non-Kikuyu Church leaders found themselves in an impossibly weak position. Being in the Kikuyus' bad books for speaking out against the government meant a great deal of frustration and even police surveillance. Nor could member Churches of the NCCK dare to be in conflict with the Council leadership which would then block their financial aid from overseas or even put them in bad odour with those in power. The Council processed and channelled most overseas funding.

Target newspaper, published jointly by the NCCK and the Christian Council of Tanzania, was a great embarrassment to the Kenya Council when it attacked the building of the KANU (Party) headquarters in Nairobi in 1968 as a misuse of funds. With the knowledge and quiet approval of NCCK, its European editor, the Revd John Schofield, was dismissed from the Board of Directors following a directive from a top government official, and the Speaker, formerly assistant editor, was appointed in his place. Surprisingly, he maintained and even carried further *Target*'s advocacy role, but he received constant reminders from the government and the Council to 'be careful' and tone down his editorials. Freedom of the press will be considered later but such pressures were not peculiar to the Church newspaper *Target*.

Kenyatta refused to attach himself to any organized religion but he believed in God and all his political speeches were full of biblical references. He maintained in his public addresses that no religion or Church, in the case of Christian denominations, was superior to others. This delighted smaller sects which continued to mushroom in Kenya. This posture was politically effective in discouraging any Church or individual from assuming an overtly prophetic role in society. Its aim was to reduce everyone to size.

In contrast to Kenyatta, President Arap Moi is a churchgoer and a member of his Africa Inland Church. He tends to worship in any Church of his choice each Sunday. He often addresses the congregation during or after worship, but this is due more to a request by Church leaders than to his own design, as his attendance is not usually prearranged.

The irony is that there have been more sharp and open conflicts between Church and state in Kenya during the time of Moi than in the time of Kenyatta. These conflicts began in 1986 after a National Pastors' Conference which passed a resolution opposing the new electoral system of 'lining up' behind candidates. The Church leadership opposed the system on the grounds that it would be divisive and dangerous for people in the armed forces, government administrators or Church leaders to show open partiality. Even university lecturers have thus far hardly participated in elections. Hence the repeated call by the National Council of Churches for the system to be abolished.

Let us look briefly at what is going on in other parts of Africa. From Kaunda of Zambia comes one of the most pointed challenges to the Church — more precisely the clergy — to take seriously their part in nation-building.

> Is not a disproportionate amount of their time and intellectual talent solely devoted to matters of domestic ecclesiastical concern? Would it be unkind of me to say that many of the clergy have completely shut themselves off from the ongoing life of our nation?[4]

Kaunda argues that as a humble Christian he is saddened by the absence of the Church's intellectual talent to stimulate discussion on great national issues. 'Both our government and nation need to have kept before them the moral and spiritual standards against which we should measure their policies and actions.'[5] But he expected only the best that the Church could offer, not tired clichés and platitudes which would be an insult to the intelligence of the people.

> Never has the Church had a more wonderful opportunity to be a relevant and effective spiritual and moral force than it has in these newly established states where persons are hungry for the truth.[6]

Adrian Hastings says of Kaunda that he has never developed an ideology or practical policy which could antagonize or alienate the Churches. 'He trusts them but also expects their close cooperation.'[7] According to Hastings, the President has regular six-monthly suppers with Church leaders, giving them a chance to consult him directly 'but the *quid pro quo* is that they never speak out in criticism in public. The Churches have been in fact gently harnessed to the ruling system and the Catholic Bishop Mulale even agreed to serve as a member of the commission for instituting a one party state.'[8]

Zambia had its share of direct confrontation between Church and state in 1968 when the youth wingers of Kaunda's United National Independence Party hounded Jehovah's Witnesses and burnt down 45 of their Kingdom Halls. Some Witnesses were killed and many more fled into the bush. Kaunda's humanism failed to extend refuge to the terribly persecuted Witnesses from Malawi in 1972 and 1975. Last year the Roman Catholic Bishop issued a pastoral letter on Peace and Justice issues in Zambia which was very critical of the human rights record in the country.

In Zimbabwe, the same Catholic Bishops have strongly criticized Mugabe for turning the country into a one-party state. Mugabe has retorted by saying that their Church is not democratic either. In the Cameroun, Guinea, Togo, Benin, Rwanda, Burundi, Uganda and Zaire terrible mental torture of Church leaders has taken place. Uganda during Amin's period was a special case and needs separate treatment. Troubles in Zaire began in October 1971 when Mobutu officially launched a manifesto known as the *Movement Populaire de la Revolution*, the Zairean philosophy of authenticity. The movement's first objective was to strengthen Mobutu's position for the task of nation-building. The urgent need, according to the document, was the decolonization of the mind: until that was achieved the life of the nation would be greatly hampered.[9] Zaireans needed to recover their soul as quickly as possible. The movement proved to have the Roman Catholic Church as the major target of

Africanization. The Catholic Church claimed to be universal, with loyalties which reached beyond the borders of Zaire. It also owed allegiance to Rome. This was unacceptable to Mobutu's philosophy of authenticity.

In January 1971, the Permanent Committee of the Roman Catholic Bishops of Zaire produced a theological statement on the Church's participation in nation-building. While recognizing the normative role of the state for organizing and managing the 'earthly kingdom', they explained that the 'Church's mission was to assist men to live according to the Gospel', serving the world and, in that particular context, the Zairean people. The statement concluded:

> Since every human society is a living organism and thus in perpetual evolution, the Church cannot link itself to a given political regime, and at the same time remain faithful to its mission.

This episode was followed by the nationalization of several Roman Catholic educational institutions, including the Catholic University of Lovanium. The President of the Conference of Bishops wrote a letter objecting, and asked for an audience with the President. The following month, Mobutu banned the use of all Christian names. In January 1972, Cardinal Malula, Archbishop of Kinshasha, was expelled from his residence, apparently for being identified with an article in a Catholic weekly which criticized the attempt to resurrect things of the past. The publication was summarily suspended.

The issue, in reality, is that the Church is the only independent organized body in Zaire and, indeed, in almost all African nations which have a one-party system of government. In such situations, the Church alone is in a position to pass independent judgement on the politics of the nation. The leaders, bent on monopolizing not only temporal but also spiritual power, view the Church with a great deal of jealousy and suspicion.

Albert Ndongmo, the Catholic Bishop of Nkongsamba in

Cameroun, was sentenced to death in 1971 for allegedly arranging a 'spiritual' coup d'état with the help of 'angels' to overthrow the government. He was not executed. Bishop Ndongmo's problem seemed to have stemmed from a bid to reconcile a tribal rebel group with the government. Sometimes bishops face the wrath of political leaders merely for having powerful international connections. This is the case in Kenya now and may have been the plight of Archbishop Tchichimbo in Sekou Toure's Guinea at about the same time as Ndongmo and Malula were facing troubles in Cameroun and Zaire. Archbishop Tchichimbo of Conakry, a leading churchman, seemed to have given no offence whatsoever save that of being an alternative source of authority (for the same reason Amin murdered the Anglican Archbishop of Uganda, Janani Luwum). Tchichimbo was sentenced to life imprisonment for taking part in a Portuguese attempt to overthrow Sekou Toure. In Liberia, Archbishop George Brown has been experiencing considerable harassment by the government in the last few years.

Nyerere has been widely considered as Africa's guru and a great original thinker on these issues. His address to the Maryknoll Sisters' Conference in New York, 16 October 1970, lays down very plainly what he perceives to be the role of the Church in nation-building. Nyerere is firmly persuaded that it is the duty of the Church to help men and women to rebel against everything which enslaves and dehumanizes them.

> But most of all, the Church must be obviously and openly fighting all those institutions and power groups which contribute to the existence and maintenance of the physical and spiritual slums — regardless of the consequences to itself or its members.[10]

If the Church kept silent on established evils, it would be identifying itself and the Christian religion with injustice. The reputation of Catholicism and the total Christian body was only redeemed by those individual servants of the Church who spoke out, even if that meant personal sacrifice. Nyerere never had a quarrel with Church leaders. He freely lectured the Churches on their role in society and they almost totally endorsed the Arusha Declaration, declaring that it was in accord with the Christian spirit and teaching on human society. They might be wrong in some specific cases, but we believe that they are right in principle.

Now, let us turn our attention to the roles which Church and state should play in the development of the human person. As we have noticed, many government functions, including political rallies, are opened with prayer. President Moi would be appalled if he addressed a meeting without praying first. The Kenya national anthem is a prayer to 'God of all creation'. Both the Tanzanian and Zambian anthems are also prayers to God to bless Africa. 'O Uganda, may God upheld thee', begins Uganda's anthem. Almost every other African national anthem includes the name of God. The Churches have produced a joint Christian Religious Educational Syllabus for all the primary and secondary schools throughout Eastern Africa. This is the first joint Catholic/Protestant syllabus in nation-wide use anywhere. The University of Nairobi has a department of Religious Studies and Philosophy. These governments employ and pay chaplains to serve in the armed forces.

Generally, exhortations in various statements concerning the Church tend to view the Church's existence and role only in terms of helping government leaders to maintain peace and stability. The Church in Africa, they imply, exists only to service the state. In this regard we should consider the following points: first, for a statesman the overriding moral dictate is the survival of the state. Stanley Hoffman says:

> Theirs is the burden of putting burdens on everyone else. Any moral statecraft has to be an ethic of consequences, in the sense of being concerned for the foreseeable effects.... It means that the good in politics is not separable from its realization.[11]

The politician thus tries to preserve the state by any means:

lying, deceiving, killing or doing evil. He believes that it is his moral imperative to do so. To him this is is not an immoral code of behaviour; to a Christian, it is.

Secondly, the missionary Church was regarded by many as part and parcel of the colonial governments in Africa. Mozambique is one of the best examples of this. African national leaders unconsciously sound as though they have replaced the colonial governments and so assumed the leadership of every institution, including the Church. Mobutu complains of the Catholic Church sticking it out when all other major institutions had given in to him. Thirdly, there is the totalitarian view of statehood in Africa. All social institutions, the Church included, must be subjected to the supremacy of the state. In Kenya the massive women's organization known as Maendeleo ya Wanawake has been affiliated to the Ruling Party, the Kenya African Nation Union. There are plans to do the same with the Central Organization of Trade Unions. Yesterday, there was a startling report in the Kenyan press that now the party wants the Kenya Law Society affiliated to it. This view has in fact been responsible for destroying the so-called ruling parties and even nationhood itself, and resulted in empire building in many countries.

The last point to remember is that national leaders are not preachers or theologians. It is therefore the duty and respon- sibility of the Church to clarify its self-understanding and its mission, and to state these strongly, clearly and repeatedly in public for everyone to understand. Far too often the agenda and tone in the task of nation-building has come from political leaders alone. The Church must move back to the centre of life and thinking of the African people in all these matters and state its case clearly. If the trumpet does not give a clear sound, no one will go to war. It should be as in the case of Prophet Amos, 'the lion has roared who will not fear' (Amos 3:8).

On the other hand there are Christians who would prefer to adopt a Calvinistic view, that because God is Lord of all there ought to be a theocratic system of government. Whenever they are faced with a problem in society they cry, 'make laws to ban it, or allow it'. They would prefer to establish a Christendom, a 'holy' nation, in which Christian ethics are enforced by state law. This view would see a separation of religious conviction from social and political life as sheer hypocrisy. This would seem to be a commendable step until we begin to realize that in a society including several religions it would be infringing the liberties of other people.

Different again are the separatist, sectarian Christians with the view that all those not for us are against us so we share no part with them. To convert society, every individual must experience the inner conversion. For this group, religion and politics do not mix. Social issues and religious matters have to be kept separate. Emphasis is put on living a life of holiness for individuals as the only means of presenting God's challenge in society. This is the predominant attitude in East Africa. This also has been the main approach to social issues in America.

Politicians fall generally into the same categories. There are those, like Nyerere and Kaunda, who want the Church to adopt a more active role in society, providing it does not make any public criticism of the political party or the national leaders. Another category of leaders regards the Church as a praying department of the government which exists only for giving divine support to the official political and economic schemes, but must keep away from politics, not only publicly, but also privately. They believe that politics is a prerogative of some people called politicians.

We must recognize that there is yet another category of people, found mainly among the intellectuals, for whom faith has no meaning. The numbers are still small but steadily growing. They hold the view that religion is absolutely irrelevant to politics and vice versa. The authentic Christian view is nevertheless one which affirms the reality and necessity of the world of politics, but demythologizes and relativizes its importance. The life of faith, hope and love cannot be established by political powers.

What then do we mean by the different roles of Church and state? Or by the contrasting statement that 'the Church is part and parcel of the government'? The answer is that the separation is institutional only, but at a different, deeper level the two are bound together in the realm of ethics by owing their origin to God. Both are established for the service of God and person. The recognition of the separation of Church and state at the institutional level must be seasoned by an equally vigorous recognition of the integrated view of life at a deeper level. Here we must work out a unified ethical perspective which gives us a vision of the unity of the whole. The reason for this is that God is the Lord over economic and political systems and not only over the Church or individual persons. Our religious ethics must speak of interpersonal love as well as social justice if there is to be a true balance. A theology which speaks only of social concerns, and neglects a deep personal faith in the risen Lord, is equally lopsided. In the integrated whole lies the oneness between Church and state, and it provides the Church with its mandate for involvement in politics.

In practical terms, separation for the Church means guaranteed freedom from interference with doctrine or ritual. State officials may not exert pressure on the appointment of Church leaders and politicians may not intrude on the inner life of the Church. Secondly, such freedom means that the Church can and should have its own financial resources and be free to determine the use of those resources. Thirdly, each national Church must be free to have contacts with other Churches. The universal nature of the Church is essential for its world mission, and must be recognized and maintained, although each Church has a responsibility to relate and be relevant to its own particular culture and political situation. There is no blueprint or ideal situation which can be transferred anywhere and everywhere. There are areas in which generalization can be made with some degree of safety, but ultimately, although there are differences which may not be permanent, each situation calls for a fresh approach by the Church in its particular context.

To the state, the separation means that there should be no interference by the Church, and that government decisions are reached through government process. The government is responsible to its citizens or the electorate, not to ecclesiastical authority. Churches and all their leaders have the right of all citizens and other institutions in the nation to exert influence on the government, but no one Church, nor any Church Council no matter how representative, has legal authority over government. Bishop John Taylor explains:

> Both Church and State are the servants of God and are responsible to Him. Neither is responsible to the other. The Church is not to be regarded as a department of the State, and the State should never be dominated by the Church. But both can, if they will, support one another in their complementary tasks.[12]

Although the Church is never part of the state, in order to express the strong African sense of the social and civil functions of religion it is very proper to hold prayers at public and civic rallies: for example, during the opening of a new session of Parliament.

Looking at various places in the world, one is bound to say that even in the USA or Great Britain, where there is an explicit statement on the subject, the Church/state relationship is still evolving, and changes continue in people's understanding of the functions and nature of the two institutions. Whether people talk of radical separation as in America, or establishment as in Britain or Sweden, all positions must be critically re-examined, particularly in the Church's constantly renewed understanding of the gospel. What does this new revelation mean to the Church's understanding of its role in the state in modern society?

The relationship of Church and state should not concentrate on the legal side. The Christian community exists within larger communities everywhere. The overriding question is the nature of the gospel and the Church's call to witness in society. This determines what the relationship of the Church to the state will be, what kind of witness the Church wishes to have in society, and what services it seeks to render.

The first and primary duty of the Church's witness is the proclamation of the Word of God. This is traditionally known as evangelism, which is the telling of the story of God in Christ, fulfilling the commission of the Lord 'to go into the world and preach the Gospel', with the aim of making disciples. The telling of this story is an inescapable mandate for the Church. It must not be viewed, however, as separate from the other forms of the Church's ministry, but as an integral part of its total mission in society. Secondly, part of that total witness is for Christians to be a community — a living, sharing and serving community. This kind of witness is visible and effective where the churches are truly open to the poor, the despised and the handicapped for whom our modern societies have little care. The Church, as a worshipping community, will certainly have minimum requirements for survival — opportunity for worship, eucharistic and other forms of fellowship, instruction and education. There are those who argue that to live wholly for the world the Church needs to de-institutionalize, but in our opinion its existence as an organic, loving community is itself a form of witness in society. Against this background of our understanding of the nature of the Church's witness and service, we must place our understanding of the nature of human society.

The modern state has expanded its authority and functions, particularly in the developing world, which regards as parastatal functions such as university education, agricultural marketing and some aspects of banking. The state assumes responsibility for its citizens in almost every department — notionally, at least, even if in fact many social services are supplemented by voluntary agencies.

Much as this national approach to the fight against poverty, disease and illiteracy is appreciated, there is the danger of state absolutism leading to idolatry. Absolutism and the idolization of leaders in Africa has in fact become demonic. But since there is no sign of this changing, the Church must decide how best to offer its ministry. Christian responsibility demands that we take the modern state seriously and recognize its status as an agency for political, social, economic and indeed religious and cultural reforms.

The mechanisms controlled by the state can become a positive force for social reform or an agency for evil repression in society. It is therefore the duty of the Church to prepare its members for responsible and effective participation in nation-building.

> The Church is the Church only when it exists for others. The Church must share in the secular problems of ordinary human life, not dominating, but helpful and serving.[13]

At this point, I wish to turn to the specific question of how the Churches contribute to Alternative Development Strategies for Africa. It is commonly understood that development should be focused on the rural sector because that is where we find the largest number of poor people, and if one is poor, one is not developed. But poverty in itself does not constitute the problem. The forces that perpetuate poverty are the real problem. These forces may be political, economic, technological or social; most often, they are found together.

The editorial of an ECA publication, *Rural Progress*, sums up the problem, thus:

> The disadvantaged segment of the rural population which is left behind in the rural areas, can hardly be expected to make the economic base of rural development more productive. Similarly, they cannot be expected to be a vocal lobby to make the ruling authorities accountable to them and establish a dialogue with them in deciding, *inter-alia*, priorities of resource allocation — especially internal, price policies and fiscal measures. They become passive and loyal 'law-abiding citizens'. The consequence is the gradual erosion of the principles of accountability. Distorted

priorities dictate resource allocation, and this largely explains the underdevelopment of Africa's rural sector today.

The rural folk are rendered powerless and marginalized from the entire development process, yet without the participation of the rural people there can be no equitable distribution of the national wealth and consequently no meaningful development.

The Church's first duty is, therefore, to address this problem by ensuring accountability on the part of political leaders while at the same time educating the community on their right to such accountability. This prophetic duty is unfortunately misunderstood by politicians to mean opposition or incitement.

Education should also be a means of enabling the people to think and do things for themselves. This is often called Development Education. Many donors now accept that for any development programme to succeed the element of education must be built into it.

It is often said that 'lack of resources, technology, infrastructure and inappropriate policies largely account for the prevalence of rural poverty in Africa'. I believe that lack of education and community organization account for rural underdevelopment because when a person is poor in mind and spirit nothing can make him rich. Enrichment of the mind and spirit can only be achieved through knowledge: when one knows what to do, how to do it, and why it has to be done.

In many African countries, development implementers discover that putting education first presents great difficulty. It is said, and rightly so, that 'a hungry man has no ears'. Given the present food situation in Africa one wonders which has to come first: food or knowledge? African countries, once self-sufficient, became food exporters and ended up dependent on food imports. Regaining self-sufficiency in food production must be placed at the top of the list in the search for alternative strategies.

Our second priority must be to find ways of blending food

production and development education if we are to get a word into the people's ears. In the past many development programmes created dependence on hand-outs, contrary to what was intended.

In spite of the fact that smallholder rural agriculture produces 80 per cent of the food and provides employment for the majority of the rural population, past policies have often ignored it. The result has been a lack of incentives for the small farmer and consequently the acceleration of rural-urban migration.

Many small-scale credit schemes do not cater for the smallholder agriculture subsector. This is a high-risk area. The problem is that the small loans given out by NGOs are not guaranteed and, therefore, the chances of default are greater. This leads the smallholder into even deeper trouble.

It is a great relief that many donors and financial institutions are beginning to come up with loan guarantee systems. It is also a great relief that African governments are favouring food subsidies for the poor consumer while raising the prices of agricultural produce. It is, however, doubtful whether these measures affect the rural poor positively though they are a burden to the economies of African countries.

The third area which should be considered is that of public health. Sick people do not make good participants in development. In this area, the Churches have been at the forefront with many mission health centres established even before Integrated Rural Development Programmes came into being.

In many developing countries public health is tied to other programmes such as water, sanitation and income-generating activities. These programmes are complementary to any successful health programme. Public health must also be community-based. The community must learn to organize and manage its own programme. This fact is increasingly accepted by major international donor and service agencies which previously favoured large-scale projects. Development must start at grassroots.

The Church has a unique structure which, if effectively utilized, can contribute enormously to development in Africa. Through this structure the Church is able to reach the entire rural population. Because of the trust and goodwill people have in its institutions, the Church network can be used to mobilize and educate. Where it is not possible for bureaucratic government institutions to reach the grassroots, the Church as a simple, people-based institution is already at the grassroots.

Institutions such as Churches and other local NGOs are in a strong position to encourage the participation of the people. Churches are the most desirable of all because they cannot be politicized. Politicization of the people's organizations makes them answerable to political masters whose development philosophy may not be people-oriented. Self-interest on the part of politicians brings about false development: development which is not sustainable because it is not based on what the people really want but on the perpetuation of political authority.

Let me finish by quoting Jesus Christ:

I came that they may have life
and have it abundantly. (John 10:10).

REFERENCES

1 Kenya Sessional Paper No. 10, p. 41.
2 *Daily Nation*, Nairobi, 22 January 1981.
3 Africa Press Service, 25 May 1981.
4 Kenneth D. Kaunda, *A Humanist in Africa*, p. 100.
5 *Ibid.*, p. 101.
6 *Ibid.*
7 Adrian Hastings, *A History of African Christianity* (Cambridge, Cambridge University Press, 1979), pp. 187 ff.
8 *Ibid.*, p. 188.
9 Ngundu Mushete, in *Christianity in Independent Africa*, p. 238.
10 Julius K. Nyerere, *Man and Development*, p. 91.

11 Stanley Hoffman, *Duties Beyond Borders* (Syracuse, Syracuse University Press, 1981), pp. 22–28.

12 John V. Taylor, *Christianity and Politics in Africa*, p. 42.

13 Dietrich Bonhoeffer, *Letters and Papers*, p. 382.

PART TWO
Background Papers

No Democracy, No Development?

Ben Turok

Democracy and Development

The *New York Times*, reporting in November 1989 on the coming Indian national elections, noted that in Bihar Province about 40 per cent of the people had never seen a ballot paper. One old man said that in all his 83 years, which included four decades of national independence and eight national elections, he had never seen the inside of a polling booth. This was because of intimidation by landlords and political bosses who manipulate the political process by means of 'booth capturing', a euphemism for fraud.

The African experience is not often as bad as this, but what is undeniable is that free voting in democratic elections is still denied to the great majority of the people. While voting is by no means the whole of democracy, it is an essential ingredient. Its absence is symptomatic of an undemocratic society.

To assist in setting the agenda for the debate on democracy and development, this paper will address three issues:

1 To what extent is democracy a central concern for Africa?
2 What kind of democracy is intended?
3 How can it be achieved?

Democratic Aspirations in Africa

It seems a long time since Africa's anti-colonial movements gathered their energies for the struggle for freedom and democracy. These two ideas were linked together on the assumption that the removal of colonial rule would usher in democratic government.

Democracy was thought to imply national liberation, to provide new opportunities for Africans to realize their full potential, untrammelled by racist discrimination and oppression. It was supposed to reflect the aspirations of the people and the mass support given to these movements.

It was also assumed that the removal of colonial rule would lead to the overcoming of the underdevelopment which had accompanied colonial exploitation. Foreign abuse of African resources would be ended and indigenous growth and development fostered.

It was soon realized, however, that the colonial powers had no intention of giving up their economic hold and that decolonization was meant to remove only the most glaring aspects of foreign control. They set about ensuring that the African personnel installed in seemingly new state institutions would be willing to allow former economic relations to persist. Others were coopted into private business to give an appearance of indigenization in the economy.

This limited adjustment was possible because the masses who had supported the struggle for independence were not sufficiently organized to ensure the full consummation of their victory. The ordinary people, who had suffered the most under colonialism, could not press their claims for a better life.

The political momentum of their struggles was first stifled by the cooling-off period while independence was 'negotiated' and leaders were manipulated into more accommodating positions. By the time independence was actually proclaimed some leaders had already backtracked substantially on earlier positions and were calling for calm and order, not to mention reconciliation. The inherited and newly created institutions bore little resemblance to the popular democracy promised earlier.

It was soon apparent that the one-sided emphasis on achieving the political kingdom without corresponding economic independence was a major weakness. The failure to speedily improve the life of ordinary people soon brought disillusionment with government and in due course serious political crisis.

Some argue that no real change was possible, no matter the intentions of the new governments, for the fundamental reason that Africa remained intractably incorporated into the world capitalist economy and its associated political order. This meant that even the formal institutions of bourgeois democracy could not take root.

Taken to its logical conclusion this means that there is no prospect for democratic change in Africa short of the fundamental transformation of the world system, a position which is unacceptable since it stifles all political aspirations and action. An alternative perspective is needed which will encourage Africa's peoples to strive to roll back the undemocratic systems to which they are subject.

A New Class

While there is no disputing the power of international capitalism to constrain and control African economies, of equal significance is the role of the domestic bourgeoisie in safeguarding foreign interests and at the same time serving their own. The new domestic dominant class adopted the development model appropriate to this function, thus ensuring the continuation of dependency while creating a base for élite accumulation.

A new state bourgeoisie came into being, taking different forms across the continent. Where there were few indigenous businesses, the main path to accumulation was through gaining office in state institutions or the main political party. Elsewhere private business served as well, particularly where a strong association was established with the state.

In general, a power bloc formed rapidly in and around the state, constituted as a state bourgeoisie. This class, which was almost entirely male, entrenched its political power and economic privileges, becoming ever more parasitic, and ensuring the further polarization of society.

The theorization of the relationship between the state bourgeoisie and the state itself remains a controversial issue in Africa. But it is generally agreed that the neocolonial state is a set of institutions through which political power is wielded by a particular class in order to exercise domination over society. However, the state may have a certain relative autonomy from this class and in some cases may even act against the interests of certain of its fractions as has happened in Zambia, Sudan and Tanzania.

It is sometimes argued that this capacity for autonomy in Africa is greater than in Europe because Africa's bourgeois classes are not so well developed. Thus the task of social cohesion and control must be exercised by the state in a more overt and direct manner. On the other hand in many countries the state itself has played a large part in creating the state bourgeoisie, e.g., in Zambia where settler rule blocked the path of African business before independence. The one-party state has been able to concentrate substantial political and economic power in the hands of a small group which uses this power parasitically.

Early promises that a single official party might work democratically by allowing a choice of candidates and debate between different political tendencies did not materialize. On the other hand, where multiple parties continued to exist as in Senegal, this has not been a condition for democracy either. Elections are conducted without proper recording of votes, parties are not allowed to supervise the counting of ballot papers, there is no freedom of organization, women do not participate, trade unions are victimized. It has become apparent that the problem of the denial of democracy is not so much a matter of form as of content. At the same time it is absolutely necessary to highlight the character of the institutions of the state and society since this will enable us to identify the mechanisms for denying democracy.

Above all, African politics remains the preserve of a tiny

sector of society. The majority of the people are still locked into subsistence agriculture, where women are predominant, and are excluded and marginalized from the national political life. Politics is the preserve of rival bourgeois factions, rudely interrupted by the interventions of the military. The African state has not become a people's state, nor does it further democracy. Indeed, most African states rapidly became distinguishable by three characteristics. Once the institutions of independence were established, the state developed an alarming indifference to the people. Very soon, the political process, which had grown up around the struggle for independence and which was brought to bear on establishing the new state, was stalled. Party branches, which had been instruments of political mobilization, became instruments for demobilization. Membership became a formal matter and officebearers increasingly the instruments of rule by the one-party state.

Finally, as real conditions of life deteriorated for the majority of the people so they were called upon to refrain from protests on the grounds that this would destabilize the system. Peace and order were said to be prerequisites for states striving for growth. Soon repression became the general condition in most African countries, with a few notable exceptions, and the military rulers were in the forefront of anti-democratic practices. Statism, in the sense of concentration of power and resources at the centre, has been an instrument of repression rather than development.

As conditions deteriorate further, of crucial importance is the lack of opportunity and space for political debate and organization such as might allow for the emergence of solutions. The scope for politics, even during elections, is limited. Where one-party states exist, opponents are not tolerated. Where a multi-party system exists, as in Senegal, the elections are a fraud. In contemporary Nigeria government proposals to create two parties of the Left and Right are a parody of democracy.

What Kind of Democracy?

As the political crisis deepens and alternatives are sought, there is a great deal of confusion about what is meant by the term democracy in Africa. For some it means the conventional parliamentary systems of Europe. For others it means a great deal more. Indeed, during the anti-colonial struggle some movements, inspired by the example of China, referred to the 'National Democratic Revolution', or 'New Democracy' which had a very different meaning to that of Europe's bourgeois democracy.

In nineteenth-century Europe the ideals of democracy were an expression of the struggle against feudalism and for the establishment of capitalism. In Africa in this century the forces engaged in the struggle for democracy were very different. They lacked that strong class cohesion which marked the bourgeoisie in other continents. We therefore must give attention to questions like: What was the mode of struggle for the establishment of the African democracy? What were the conditions for the actual transfer of power? What was the political programme of the anti-colonial movements? What power groups were in contest within these movements? Which were the main social forces engaged in the struggle? Which played the leading role? What formal institutions did they inherit? And what were the international conditions at the time?

Political Form

Probably the main factor in determining the form of democracy was the character of the handover of political power. Since this was 'negotiated' between a powerful imperialist state and an ill-organized though often rebellious popular force, the conditions for transfer were set by the former, blunting the impetus for national liberation.

But the evidence is overwhelming that Africa was not 'ripe'

for the Westminster model of parliamentary democracy either. The various parties that existed were not sufficiently differentiated on the basis of distinct interests; instead they represented rival personalities and factions. Crucially, with some notable exceptions like Sudan, the peasants, workers, urban poor and middle strata had been unable to create their own distinct political organizations (apart from some trade unions which were mainly concerned with work conditions) and therefore were unable to constitute a distinct force in the post-independence line-up. In other words the social forces were not yet organized to form the democratic content in the political shell. In addition, the avowed anti-imperialism of the independence movements was seriously undermined by the collaborationist posture of many political leaders.

The hollow shell of democracy coupled with the absence of real social content meant that there was little change in the economy. While many state enterprises were set up, and many foreign firms nationalized, the fundamental character of the economy remained unchanged. There were variations on the neocolonial formula: state capitalism, mixed economy, free enterprise capitalism. In each case foreign control remained powerful though generally indirect. Since development was seen to be a state project, bringing little benefit for the peasants and ordinary people, it aroused little enthusiasm after the novelty of independence wore off.

This conference will probably agree that democracy is not an end in itself. Democracy is a concept of society and is about how its resources are used and distributed. This implies a development strategy which will overcome underdevelopment and benefit the people. It is certainly not to be found in some ideal type, nor is it necessarily based on the 'Westminster' style of government, or limited by the conceptions espoused in the bourgeois revolutions of nineteenth century Europe. Africa has its own needs and it must set its own democratic agenda.

The Road to Democracy and Development

Africa, having lost its way to both democracy and development, badly needs new initiatives and perspectives. First, we must seek to redress the abuses of human rights which have derailed democracy in so many countries. Second, we should fight to establish on firm ground the civil rights promised to our peoples, including freedom of the press, freedom of political expression and organization, freedom to press for the rights of workers, women, and all the disadvantaged sectors of society. But it must be made clear that these conditions will not only be fulfilled for those already in a position to take advantage of them, but also for the ordinary people.

The problem seems to be that presently these masses are not organized to a degree where they could benefit from any simple opening of political space. The political communities of traditional African society have been sorely disrupted by colonialism and urbanization. There do not now exist on a substantial scale autonomous social organizations independent of the state such as can exert pressure in the interests of the disadvantaged classes. Contemporary experience throughout the world seems to reinforce the view that such organizations are essential as conveyor belts for popular interests as well as checks to authoritarian and self-serving rule by bureaucrats and élites generally. Even the existence of professional associations of doctors and lawyers, as well as the press, has been shown, in Nigeria for example, to be of enormous value in constraining authoritarianism.

We will also probably agree that a development strategy is not a technical matter of fine tuning here or there, of adjusting what exists in a technocratic way. Development strategy is a matter of politics and therefore a function of democracy in form as well as content. This implies that aspirations to democracy must be linked to development within a single project. Neither can stand on its own and neither can be meaningful separately. Indeed many writers now refer to the need for social transformation meaning a fundamental change in the conditions of production and social relations for the mass of the people: as long as scarcity and poverty predominate there can be no meaningful democracy or development. These are the objective conditions necessary for a new life for the people as opposed to the state personnel, the bourgeoisie and external interests such as multinationals, the IMF and the World Bank.

Others argue that only the socialist road can open up such prospects. This is not the place to resolve this issue except to say that the crisis in Africa is of such a scale that it would seem appropriate to propose a set of policies likely to unite a spectrum of society broad enough to bring major changes while yet keeping the basic requirements of development and democracy on the agenda. As many others have found in the contemporary world, the issue of unity around democratic and development perspectives precedes that of socialism.

How to Get There?

The post-independent state in Africa has proved to be adept at silencing opposition by a variety of means. There have been the more obvious methods of liquidating the opposition, coercing critics, suppressing freedoms, but also the cooption of potential opponents. In several countries where there is no open political space for opposition, governments have managed to induce intellectuals to participate in official institutions, many agreeing to do so in the belief that it is only possible to win change by working from inside the system. But is it possible to accept such positions and yet maintain a principled stand on the issues of democracy and development? This problem faces many intellectuals across Africa.

In other countries opposition forces accept the agenda set by the state because the alternative is to have no opportunities at all. This can lead to a false sense of democratic openings becoming available when this is simply cosmetic. On the other hand it is possible to take up an ultra-left position, eschewing all opportunities on the grounds that full democracy is not being restored. Where lies the balanced view?

How can the disparate interests of youth, women, workers, peasants and professionals be coordinated into a united effort advancing the interests of all? What kind of coalition can be built in the process of struggle and what kind of perspective can be advanced to ensure that each sector will see its own interests furthered in any new system which might emerge? What can be said of the Sudanese proposals that there should actually be a coalition whereby professional groups, trade unions, army, women, youth have direct representation in government which rules on the basis of consensus, protecting the common interests of all these forces? Would such a system make possible the implementation of real participatory democracy, which has become a cliché of post-independence Africa? Can we sustain popular power which coexists with state power? Can we teach governments to respect the tension between democratic claims and the centralizing needs of government?

Critics need to set about working through some of these proposals and treating them as substantive policy measures which stand a chance of gaining popular support. For socialists there is the added challenge of how socialist democracy differs from other conceptions of democracy and whether the vast contortions in Eastern Europe should influence their thinking for Africa. In particular they need to address at least four issues:

- How can we build people's power which is distinct from, yet in combination with, state power, in a concerted effort for development?
- How can civil society maintain its mass organizations, independent of the state but without contradictions with it?
- How can powerful leaders be persuaded to maintain a simple lifestyle, be constrained from authoritarianism and from abusing their power for personal or state reasons?
- How can we ensure that government is humane and avoids arbitrary action, no matter the difficulties encountered?

The African Debt Crisis: Which Way Out?

E. N. Maganya

Alongside the epic unfolding of the great debt crisis, with its cost of big spenders, like Mexico, Brazil and Argentina a second, low-budget drama has been played out in the Third World. The protagonists are small debtors, low income countries, mostly African (Westlake, 1985).

Introduction

One of the most striking features of the African debt is that its small volume relative to that of the highly indebted middle-income countries should be attended by the most 'exasperating and excruciating' debt service obligations (OAU, 1987).

While the amount of debt for 1980–85 and 1987 for all developing countries and the highly indebted countries increased from US$604.2 billion and US$299.7 billion to US$886.0 billion and US$420.8 billion respectively, that of Sub-Saharan Africa (SSA) increased from US$58.3 billion to US$100.3 billion. It should be noted that the amount of debt for the highly indebted countries (most Latin American countries) by 1987 was almost four times that of SSA. In other words, in volume terms, Latin American countries are more indebted than SSA.

This overall figure of the degree of indebtedness does not actually show the gravity of the debt-servicing problems of SSA and the African continent in general. It should be noted that the debt service ratio increased from 24.0 per cent in 1975 to 37.7 per cent in 1986 for all the highly indebted countries and from 10.2 per cent to a very high level of 76.2 per cent for the low-income African countries during the same period. The debt service ratio for the SSA was almost twice that of the highly indebted countries. Figures for the debt-GNP ratio show the same trend. This increased from 18.1 per cent in 1975 to 55.9 per cent in 1987 for the first group of countries and from 25.2 to 76.2 per cent for the second group of countries.

Another important manifestation of the debt crisis is the phenomenon of the reverse flow of resources. The 1980s have witnessed an unprecedented flow of resources from developing countries to developed industrial countries, thus making the prospects for economic recovery bleak. The reality of the reverse flow of resources has been acknowledged even by the World Bank and the IMF. According to the IMF (April, 1989), while there was a positive net transfer of resources of about US$147 billion through long term lending (including concessional loans) between 1977 and 1982 to the developing countries, the period after 1982 witnessed a substantial reverse transfer of resources of US$85 billion.

Perhaps even more instructive is the fact that between 1982 and 1987 the highly indebted middle-income countries have transferred more financial resources than they ever received in the period 1978—82. They transferred US$92 billion against US$61 billion.

Even SSA, borrowing on highly concessional terms from official lenders (mainly multilateral and bilateral institutions) was forced to transfer to the IMF between 1986 and February 1987 three and a half times the resources received in 1985. The net outflow of resources was equal to US$1 billion.

The above statistical presentation demonstrates the debt crisis of developing countries with specific reference to the African situation. There seems to be unanimity amongst both debtors and creditors that the debt crisis is a real one and that urgent and effective corrective policy measures are needed in order to avoid a collapse of the debtors' economies which would obviously have a negative impact on the financial markets of developed industrial countries. What is controversial, however, are the reasons that led to the debt crisis and economic strategies for solving the crisis.

The Causes of the African Debt Crisis

Without a correct understanding of the causes that led to the outbreak of the African debt crisis in the early 1980s, it will be difficult to prescribe correct socio-economic and political strategies for economic recovery.

There have been three main positions in the analysis of the economic crisis whose manifestation is the ongoing debt crisis. The *first* position is that which seeks to understand the causes of the crisis as having originated from internal dynamics. This internalist position has been clearly summarized in what is now known as the Berg Report (World Bank, 1981).

Those who hold this position emphasize the inappropriate nature of the domestic policies of most African countries particularly, in the following areas:

1 inadequate producer prices particularly for export crops;
2 the grossly overvalued exchange rate that made imports cheaper and exports expensive;
3 chronic budgetary deficits which were in part caused by inefficient state-owned marketing institutions, inappropriate and ineffective subsidies and unnecessary investments in welfare sectors.

Structural Adjustment Programmes formulated on the basis of this analysis are based on demand-switching (away from non-tradeables to tradeables) and demand-restricting policies. The main objective is to restore external balance through increased exports and internal balance by removing or greatly reducing budgetary deficits. These policies have by and large governed most of the SAPs now being undertaken by over 30

SSA countries, as the price they must pay for financial assistance from the donor community.

It can be seen that the internalists play down external factors such as falling commodity prices or the protectionist and monetary policies of the developed countries. Moreover, the undue emphasis put on balancing the books, plays down the human factor as the most critical aspect of the development process. The implication of these omissions will be dealt with at greater length later in this paper.

The second position is that of the economic and political analysts who emphasize externalities as the most imporant causes of the African economic crisis. The unequal terms of trade, mainly explained by ever-declining commodity prices and increasing tariff and non-tariff barriers, are given as the most important explanatory factors of the crisis. Those who hold this position are mainly the African leaders. for whom it is much more convenient to externalize the causes of the African crisis. The much more difficult analytical exercise of comprehending the crisis as having been brought about by the dynamic interaction of internal and external factors, with the latter exercising the dominant role, is conveniently avoided.

Common to the two approaches is the economism that dominates all the arguments and prescriptions. More aid conditional on increased primary exports is presented as the most effective solution and seems plausible to most African leaders. The rather complex political structures and cultural profiles that have been built over time as the articulation of the capitalist mode of production, and have now been affected by the ongoing crisis, are not subjects of serious analysis from the point of view of the political economy.

In our opinion, the most recent policy re-thinking by the ECA (ECA 1987) on the African crisis has tried to break out of the strait jacket of economism and eclectic analyses. The crisis is seen as having been caused by both internalities and externalities, although the latter plays a dominant role. Likewise, it is not merely an economic crisis that can be solved by the simple exercise of balancing the books. The African economic crisis is economic, political and cultural; above all, it has tended to demobilize social groups that are supposed to carry the bigger burden of restructuring the African economies. This complex understanding of the African crisis demands suitably complex solutions.

Which Way Out?

We shall now try to provide alternative development strategies that will, we hope, provide long term solutions to the debt crisis. In doing so, we shall begin with the conventional debt-solving strategies. The objective of doing so will be to show why these strategies cannot work, whether in the short or the long term.

Conventional debt-solving strategies

Conventional debt-solving strategies have been based on one important but wrong assumption — that with economic recovery in the developed industrial countries, there will be more demand for the commodities of the developing countries. Increased earnings from developing countries' exports will therefore enable them to pay part or the whole of the debt. Given this background, the emphasis put on increased exports by SAPs is not surprising.

Both the 'involuntary' lending by private banks to Latin American countries and the plethora of debt-relieving measures for SSA have an element of 'buying time' until things get better in the world market. We shall not go into the details of all the debt-relieving measures undertaken by the IMF, the World Bank and the donor community, as these have been dealt with elsewhere. Let it suffice to point out that the debt reschedulings at the Paris Club which have been accompanied by the carrot and stick policies of 'highly' concessional new loans and the 'export-led' policies of the SAPs are all based on the flawed assumption that the end of recession in the developed countries will mean expanded markets for the commodities of the developing countries.

The recent behaviour of the world market, however, does not bear these assumptions out. Indeed, the recovery of the economies of the major industrial countries of the West has not been followed by increased imports from the developed countries. As correctly observed by Doumou (1989, p. 18):

> Contrary to the previous period, from 1980 Third World exports dropped by nearly 25%. This resulted in a reduction in the share taken by Third World exports of world exports, which dropped from 33.6% in 1980 to 24.5% in 1986. Within world trade, South-South trading has continued to deteriorate since 1982 and has declined almost to its 1955 level (6.6% in 1985).

This new behaviour of the world market is a reflection of two related developments: *one*, the emergence of a New International Division of Labour (NIDL) based on the monopoly of input-saving technologies by the developed countries; and *two*, the regionalization of economic and monetary relations.

The monopolization of input-saving technologies in the form of information technology makes the promotion of the export-led growth strategy on the basis of primary commodity export highly questionable. Increased exports of primary commodities are not only being blocked by the high tariff and non-tariff barriers now being erected at an alarmingly rapid rate by the developed industrial countries, but more so by the ever-decreasing volume of inputs from primary commodities per unit of product.

The negative consequences of the protectionist and irresponsible subsidy policies of the developed countries on the participation of the developing countries in international trade has been commented upon by World Bank thus:

> Approaches to the debt problem pursued during the past few years have increasingly focused attention more sharply

on the links between industrial country performance — including trade policy, as well as GDP growth — and the scope for developing countries to increase exports and achieve economic growth. The revival of protectionism, particularly noticeable since the early 1980s, remains disquieting. While agriculture has been widely protected for many years, the fall in international prices has often not been matched by equal reductions in domestic support prices.... This has led to a sharp scissors effect. Not only has the cost of protection risen, but the ever more tightly closed markets and subsidized exports have exerted downward pressure on already low international market prices for agricultural commodities (World Bank, 1988).

The increasingly protectionist policies of the developed industrial countries must be analysed within the context of another new development — the regionalization of markets and currencies, a development that is definitely going to marginalize the developing world, and particularly the African continent, even further. The expected integration of the markets and currencies of the EEC countries by the year 1992 is going to increase the protectionist policies of the developed western countries, contrary to the rather optimistic and misguided interpretation of the April 1989 IMF Report. Assessing the outlook for the world economy up to 1995, the IMF makes the following interesting comment:

Steps towards further integration and internal liberalization are currently envisaged in the EC by 1992. This could make an important contribution to longer term economic revival in industrial countries (IMF, April 1989, p. 38).

While internal liberalization will indeed strengthen the economy of Europe, this will not necessarily lead to more liberalized trade practices, nor will the expected long-term revival of the economies of industrial countries have any positive impact on the economies of the developing countries. In fact, internal liberalization means more internal trade and that whatever external trade might take place is residual. This is the logic of economic integration. Woe to the countries that still believe in the myth of export-led growth on the basis of one or a few countries! As we move towards the end of the twentieth century 'internal liberalization' or, if you wish, internally based export-led growth on the basis of regional, continental or sub-continental economic integration will dominate international trade relations.

Regional integration and popular participation: the two pillars of effective economic recovery for Africa

In our discussion we have deliberately avoided the more technical aspects of debt reduction measures. These, we believe, will continue to be important for both the debtor and creditor countries. The struggle to roll over the payment of both interest and principal at lower interest rates; partial or total cancellation of debt by the creditors; the current willingness of the creditor countries to offer new aid at extremely concessional rates for SSA (the Enhanced Structural Adjustment Facility, the Special Programme of Assistance, etc.); even attempts by some debtor countries to declare moratoria on part of their debt — all these are important but palliative.

POPULAR PARTICIPATION AND ECONOMIC RECOVERY PROGRAMMES

It should be emphasized that in the 1970s the developed countries, through multilateral institutions, extended a lot of concessional loans to SSA and yet, as we all now know, these have resulted in the current debt crisis. In most cases, these loans were contracted by extremely unpopular regimes or 'benevolent' states who thought they had the right to contract loans on behalf of their people. What is even more disturbing, however, is the fact that the policy framework within which the loans were to be used was, almost invariably, determined by the creditors.

Tanzania, the major recipient of concessional loans per capita in Africa, is a case in point. Most of the economic policies formulated and undertaken in the 1970s were either formulated by the World Bank or had its direct backing. The policy of devolving the bureaucracy from the centre to the periphery, otherwise known as the Decentralization Policy of 1972, the massive spatial concentration of households (Villagization Programme) and the subsequent statization of the marketing institutions created an ideal situation for the realization of McNamara's new-found love for the rural poor.

The result of all these policies was increased marginalization of the peasants from the development process and a significant contribution to the fall in production of both export and food crops in Tanzania, particularly after 1979.

With the onset of the current crisis and the acceptance by over 30 SSA countries of SAPs since 1982, the lessons of the 1970s seem not to have been well grasped. Most of the stand-by agreements signed between the African governments and the IMF have acquired the character of top secrets. Essential details of the deals are not even made known to the members of parliament and open and critical discussions of the negative aspects of SAPs evokes the wrath of the instruments of coercion of the state — as has been demonstrated in Nigeria.

Perhaps even more disturbing is the authoritarian nature of the macro-economic policies that inform the SAPs. The obsession with balancing the books through such measures as budgetary cuts of social services (education and health services, etc) or removal of food and input subsidies seems to have replaced any process of dialogue. The magic power of the rules of supply and demand are supposed to do the trick. It cannot be overemphasized that popular participation is an important aspect of the market place.

Lastly, a word or two once more on the important question of regional integration. It is important to re-iterate the point that economic regionalism is increasingly becoming an important feature of the international economic system. This is contrary to the simplistic notion of 'one world' now increasingly gaining popularity. The notion of the 'one world' must be closely tied to that of regionalism. Those countries which will be able to tap the advantages of economic regionalism will be able to participate effectively in the 'one world' and those that will not will increasingly be marginalized from it. As we move into the twenty-first century, the African continent has two alternatives — to condemn itself to perpetual poverty or to begin the long and difficult process of establishing a viable regional economic and currency integration.

BIBLIOGRAPHY

ECA, *African Alternative Framework to Structural Adjustment Programmes for Socio-Economic Recovery and Transformation* (Addis Ababa, 1987).

IMF, *World Economic Outlook* (Washington, April 1989).

——, *Africa's External Debt Problem, Meeting of Intergovernmental Experts on Finance and Monetary Questions* (addis Ababa, November 1987).

N. E. Maganya, 'The Third World debt, its servicing and prospects for sustainable economic growth', paper presented to the National Conference on 'Tanzania, Debt Problems and the World Economy', Dar es Salaam, 29–30 June 1989.

N. E. Maganya and H. Othman, *The Debt Problem in the Context of the Third World: The Case of Tanzania* (Institute of Development Studies, Dar es Salaam, and Institute of African Alternatives, London, 1988).

OAU, *African Common Position on Africa's External Debt Crisis* (Addis Ababa, 1987).

OCDE, *Development Cooperation* (Paris, 1988).

Samir, Amin, 'In favour of a polycentric world', keynote address to the African Regional Conference of the Society for International Development, Nairobi, November 1989.

South Commission, *Statement on External Debt* (1987).

Westlake, M., 'Debt drama on a low budget', *South*, February 1985.

The World Bank, *World Bank Development Report, 1988*, (Washington, OUP, 1988).

BACKGROUND PAPER

Alternatives For African Women

Mary Turok

Five Years After the Decade of Women

A crisis of unparalleled proportions is facing Africa. In its course the progress of women has faltered and the movement for equality has been set back. It is time to take stock and re-examine the goals and strategies set by the Decade for Women.

The Decade was not the first United Nations initiative on women. Women's equality has been enshrined in many UN documents since the adoption of the Universal Declaration of Human Rights in 1948. During the Decade the Convention on the Elimination of All Forms of Discrimination against Women was adopted by the General Assembly and by the end of the Decade 93 member countries had signed it and 73 had ratified or acceded to it. Yet equality has not been realized, even in countries which signed or ratified this convention.

The Decade of Women gave legitimacy to women's hopes, presenting women's condition as the concern of society as a whole. It encouraged and strengthened women's struggles for recognition and for greater control of their lives. New ideas and activities were opened up. But, while more research and information on women led to increased resources and opportunities for some, this did not lead to the development of coherent gender-sensitive programmes.

Heightened international consciousness and a new sense of solidarity among women emerged during the Decade. And as awareness and militancy grew, thousands of new organizations were established. But this new consciousness was not connected to the material roots of women's subordination, nor did it sufficiently penetrate beyond the arena of women's movements. The conditions of most women deteriorated during the Decade.

Over 2,000 delegates, the majority women, from over 150 countries represented their governments at the Nairobi conference in July 1985. The Non-Governmental Forum which preceded it was attended by 14,000 representatives of women's organizations, the majority of them from neighbouring African countries and the developing world. Both meetings adopted the document, *Forward Looking Strategies*. The scene seemed set for the advance of a world wide movement for change.

Five years have now passed since the historic Nairobi conference. In anticipation of the five-yearly monitoring due in 1990, the Institute for African Alternatives is taking the opportunity to look at the goals and strategies set by *Forward Looking Strategies* to ensure that equality was implemented and guaranteed by the year 2000. To what extent do they reflect the present needs and concerns of women in Africa? We also wish to propose ways in which these goals might be concretized and elaborated in order to become more relevant in the present crisis.

New Directions

Forward Looking Strategies set three objectives for women: Equality, Development and Peace.

Equality

Earlier this century, the key to equality for women was thought by many to lie in the vote, in legal rights and in access to education and employment. The Decade of Women contributed to the extension of the concept of equality by linking discrimination against women with factors operating at family, community, national and international levels.

Equality in law was not the panacea. If women were to participate fully in society they had to have the opportunities to exercise their rights and develop their skills and talents. But *Forward Looking Strategies* failed to address two important issues: the effect of culture, tradition and religion on women's rights and their power to exercise them, and the potential of women's organizations to challenge backward beliefs and practices.

While the document repeatedly called upon governments to extend equality to women, in its preoccupation with individual rights it overlooked the many roles of women's organizations: educating women on their rights, helping them to confront their daily experiences of subordination, mobilizing women to pressurize governments and facilitating power-sharing. It thus left out of account one of the main achievements of the Decade: the generation of women's organizations.

Development

Development was recognized during the Decade as a precondition for women's achievement of equality, and mistaken development strategies were acknowledged as having increased inequality and poverty. Obstacles to women's participation in development were identified: child and household responsibilities, traditional attitudes, poverty, the worsening economic situation and the lack of political will.

Some of the strategies proposed for removing these obstacles were the following: eliminating gender bias, sharing parental responsibilities, ending employment discrimination, recognizing women's contribution in food production, improving access to health care and education. This was a start. But there was a disappointing absence of concrete or programmatic strategies which could be integrated into national development programmes. In the absence of such guidelines there was a real danger that official recognition of women's disadvantaged position, prompted by the Decade of Women, would fade.

Peace

Forward Looking Strategies developed the concept of peace by widening the conventional definition and including sexism, which reinforced hostile attitudes between the sexes, among the obstacles to peace. It called for priority to be given to the elimination of domestic violence and violence against women. A strong call was made to governments to halt the arms race and divert these resources to development and improvement in the situation of women.

But while calling for the participation of women and for their mutual support in conflict situations, the general thrust of strategies to achieve peace are targeted at governments, as though they were the only force on the international stage. There is no call for movements and organizations to pressurize governments into ending wars and armed conflicts.

Shortcomings of the Decade: Feminism and Politics

Forward Looking Strategies is a detailed chronicle of the inequalities experienced by women. But it does not focus on the primary obstacles to women's advance nor does it identify the principal objectives of women's liberation. Global as women's subordination may be, women of different classes, nations and worlds have different priorities.

The assumptions of the document are that women's interests are the same by virtue of their common gender and that women will advance through the goodwill of governments or the intervention of successful women. This seems to reflect the emphasis on individual solutions which has characterized the feminist movement in the West. In our opinion it is unhelpful in developing appropriate strategies for the achievement of gender equality, especially in Africa. While we recognize feminism as one of the great movements for progress in our time, the positions taken by significant sections of the women's liberation movement in recent years seem to be unhelpful to the achievement of women's emancipation.

The labour movement in the West has a poor record on women's rights. Women were accepted as members and activists but their needs and demands were for a long time ignored. This led to women turning to separatist struggles. Inspired by the radical school of feminism which declared man to be the main enemy of women's emancipation, a preoccupation with gender oppression developed which dissociated women's struggles from other movements for social change. This preoccupation with a common identity as women left politics out of account. The women's movement became intolerant of diversity and insensitive to class and ethnic differences. This led to further fracturing.

The declaration that the personal is political and the campaigns on abortion, rape and domestic violence which it gave rise to heightened public awareness of women's oppression in the social and inter-personal spheres. But, sadly, they did not move beyond this to wider political issues. Had the perception of this important dimension of women's oppression been focused on women empowering themselves to participate more confidently and effectively in social change in general and the struggle for gender equality in particular it would have been a far more positive contribution to progress.

Legal advances have enabled many individual women to make strides towards social equality and equal pay, but their progress has further blurred the goals of the feminist movement. Most women, still hampered by poor education, lack of training and childcare responsibilities, are not in a position to take advantage of equal opportunities. Advances by prominent women are used by the media to undermine the collective struggle, to disguise the continuing disadvantage of most women and to support the myth that the post-feminist age has arrived.

We are of the opinion that the advance of women has been slowed down by the absence of a coherent women's movement and that, despite differing material conditions and histories, there is a need to sustain solidarity, to share problems and solutions, to find ways of working together and to develop a thorough analysis of women's oppression.

Lack of Progress in Africa

Of special concern to IFAA is the lack of progress towards equality on the African continent and the urgent need for clear programmes and strategies and for a better understanding of the roots of women's subordination.

In pre-colonial African society, women as child-bearers had primary responsibility for children and the home, but this role was highly valued and they also played important and necessary roles in social and economic activities. Colonialism disrupted the subsistence economies, opening the way to cash crops, the marginalization of women from the wider economy and the devaluation of their domestic roles. Independence brought legal rights to men and women and the process of women's emancipation appeared to have started.

Sustainable development could only be achieved with the full participation of women, concluded the ECA's fourth regional conference on Women and Development, yet laws which discriminated against women still existed, women continued to be under-represented in secondary and higher education, were largely absent from scientific and technical training programmes, and played little part in decision-making, management and the political process (Abuja Declaration, 1989).

Current statistics attest that in Africa women represent 60 per cent of the workforce but earn only 10 per cent of the cash income. Many women work an eighteen-hour day but few own livestock or the land they work on. Even in countries where women have achieved formal equality they still do not share equally in the ownership of land, tools or livestock, nor do they have any control over income from the sale of crops.

The lives of many women are still dominated by tradition. Hazardous practices such as early marriage and pregnancy, female circumcision, nutritional taboos, inadequate child spacing and unprotected deliveries are still current realities in many African countries and little progress has been achieved in their abolition (Abuja Declaration, 1989).

The Effects of Debt and Structural Adjustment on Women

The collapse of commodity prices, external borrowing and the burden of debt repayments have led to the acceptance by most African governments of the SAPs of the World Bank and the IMF. These are having a crippling effect on overall African development, often undermining long-term government commitments to improving people's lives. Most women's work is not acknowledged in national accounts and structural adjustment programmes tend to take it for granted that shortfalls in welfare services will be made good by women's invisible labour.

An important feature of SAPs is massive devaluation of national currencies. This has led to severe cuts in government spending on health, education and other services. Child immunization programmes have declined due to clinic closures and lack of vaccines. According to the WHO, this has led to the re-emergence of diseases previously thought to have been eradicated. Child mortality has ceased to decline and is rising in some countries. Women's use of antenatal and delivery care is also falling. Fertility levels remain high and one in 21 African women die as a result of pregnancy. Maternal mortality rates are between 30 and 200 times the rates in industrial countries and are almost certainly rising.

Spending on education is falling — in some countries fees have been introduced. Elsewhere there has been no expansion and the excess demand is absorbed by private schools. Poor families are having to choose between food and children's education. Girls' education is hardest hit. Adult women, with the highest rate of illiteracy, have been hit by cuts in literacy programmes.

Programmes to extend access to clean water, which would reduce water-borne diseases and lessen the burden on women and girls of carrying water over long distances, have been held up. In some countries existing water reticulation is no longer fully operational and women are again carrying water.

Trade liberalization is another feature of adjustment programmes. This is intended to help crop production for the market but it has not helped rural women, putting them under increased pressure to produce cash crops, often without wages and at the cost of household food production and child care.

Retrenchment in the public sector, privatization and the removal of government subsidies on food and transport are other features of adjustment programmes. They have led to price rises and increased unemployment. Food prices have risen fastest, forcing poor households to restrict food consumption. World Bank estimates show caloric supplies in many countries to be from 68 per cent to 91 per cent of minimum requirements.

Unemployment rose by 8 per cent between 1980 and 1985, according to the ILO, and the dependency ratio is nearly 3 persons to every one employed. In urban areas women, with the main responsibility for feeding families, have been forced to extend their income-generating activities. Largely excluded from formal occupations by convention or poor education, many more women have moved into the sphere of small trade, home brewing and prostitution.

Effects of Environmental Degradation on Women

Eighty-eight per cent of rural African women work in agriculture.

They produce, process and market 80 per cent of total food production. It has been estimated that to transport water, fuel and goods from source to market a woman spends between 2,000 and 5,000 hours a year, the equivalent of an eight-hour day job. There is little time or effort left for environmental protection.

Poor women are the hardest hit by the degradation of their environment, from which they extract their meagre livelihood. Many must travel further and further to find water and fuel. Yet economic policies continue to overlook women's central role in development and in preserving and sustaining the environment.

New Perspectives: Feminism in Africa

The term feminist in Europe and America has been attributed to women who rebel against inequality. This has not been the case in Africa where it is widely held that feminism is an imported idea and any African woman who calls herself a feminist is accused of betraying her culture: the oppression of both men and women was a result of colonial conquest and ended with independence. In rejecting feminism, most of those who oppose women's emancipation single out the ideas of radical feminists who see man as the main enemy. They then use this to dismiss the legitimacy of women's claims.

Women in Africa have long recognized that their sub-ordination to men was not the effect of colonialism alone, but many contemporary women's organizations were generated as part of national liberation movements. Women were seen as a sector to be organized towards the strategic end of independence. Differences in the interests of men and women were played down in the common cause. This experience shaped the conceptualization of women's oppression and the objectives of their struggles.

Governments in Africa often try to absorb women's organizations, in much the same relationship as existed in national liberation movements. When this fails the organizations may be banned or the government may substitute their own official women's organization. These are often well-funded but seldom become grassroots organizations. Their main activity is supporting the government on official occasions.

The feature common to most African women's organizations, conservative and radical, is that they are political and work hand in hand with other political forces. In this respect they differ markedly from many Western feminist groups. Currently women's organizations in Africa take the following forms:

1 Progressive women's organizations which challenge the subordinate position of women, sometimes working underground.
2 Liberal women's organizations which concentrate on the achievement of legal equality.
3 Conservative women's organizations which are opposed to women's liberation and concerned with the propagation of traditional beliefs and practices.
4 Women's organizations that have developed spontaneously in response to a crisis or around single issues.
5 Women's organizations formed in response to international aid agencies or NGOs seeking to promote development which is inclusive of women.

Women and Development: Some Proposals

There is a pressing need for women's integration in development to be spelled out in well-designed implementation strategies in every sphere of public activity. Actual strategies cannot be left to the experts, to economists or lawyers, without women having the opportunity to articulate their needs.

They must act as a significant pressure group to promote enlightened policy, attitudinal changes and recognition . . . .
The mobilization of women for development is not just a question of equity but of economic efficiency (Abuja Declaration, 1989).

Sustainable development policies should aim at releasing women from some of their burdens and at giving them access to education, training and health care. This would raise their stature and confidence, enable them to participate more fully in the social, cultural and political spheres and endow them with the will and perspective to change their lives and society.

If progress towards equality is to be sustained a number of questions need to be monitored: women's access to land, to credit and to legal and family planning services; and the impact of harmful customary practices. To this end the following steps are proposed:

1 The establishment of a documentation centre in Africa.
2 The development of information packages for women on their rights.
3 The production and dissemination of information on technical skills to rural women.
4 The holding of seminars for men on women's rights.
5 The recording of survival strategies so women can learn from one another.
6 The preparation of information on the harmful effects of traditional practices and its dissemination to parents.

We suggest that ultimately development can only be achieved with the transformation of society. Development is more than growth and concerns the quality of life and just distribution between classes and sexes. It cannot be defined outside the orbit of politics and the only guarantee of development for women and the poor in Africa will be democracy.

The Need for a Fresh Start

1 We believe that the movement for equality for women should go beyond reducing inequalities. Most of the world's women are poor, black and workers. Hence the struggle against sexual oppression is one component of the larger

struggle to transform society and establish a new social order.

2   Because of the interrelation between sexual oppression and class and race oppression, women's equality can only be guaranteed in a society in which all men and women enjoy human rights, democracy and freedom from exploitation and domination.

3   Experience has taught us that individual rights are easily lost without power. In order to consolidate their gains and to win greater power women need independent organizations which will strive for a greater role in politics, the economy, society and the cultural domain. The struggle for equality must be pursued at every level: personal, group, community and societal.

4   The major obstacle to effective equality is not oppression by individual men, but women's disproportionate responsibility for the home and for social reproduction. The women's movement should campaign for domestic work to be recognized as productive work, for its sharing with men and children, and for a shorter working week for all.

5   There should be a shift from exclusive concern with production towards the idea of a social wage which would make provision for preventive health, maternity and other services for the benefit of women. Greater communal responsibility and cooperation should be fostered.

6   A woman's potential and scope as a human being should not be in conflict with her destiny as a woman. All women should have access to productive and creative work in society. The development of material conditions for women's full participation in all areas of social life should be a priority.

7   Feminist thought should become a liberating theology, shared by men and women. Ideologies that belittle, humiliate and seclude women should be challenged and exposed.

8   The capacity for human love must be developed as an act of courage and commitment to others. Intimate relations

between men and women should no longer be based on domination, submission and fear.

9   As a result of the transformation of domestic labour and relations between the sexes, a higher form of the family should emerge based on equality, justice and real affection. The generational cycle of disrespect and exploitation of women would then be broken.

10 All the struggles, yearnings and aspirations of women should be translated into a Charter of Women's Rights and women should press for its adoption and implementation by governments and by all formal and informal organiz-ations, institutions and associations.

POSTSCRIPT

In writing this paper I have drawn on the ideas of Nawal el Sa'daawi, Fatima Barbiker Mahmoud, Jo Beale, Ben Turok, Mohamed Suliman and others to whom I wish to express my gratitude.

BACKGROUND PAPER

Sustainable Development Strategies for Africa

Mohamed Suliman

The Pre-colonial Situation

For countless centuries African people have maintained a living balance with their natural environment and the resources on which they depend. They kept up an intimate, organic relationship with nature, characterized by a high degree of sensitivity and respect for the workings of natural ecosystems, an almost sacred limit to exploitation and sense of duty to conservation. Controls and taboo systems were a manifestation of this sense of close relatedness between Africans and their surroundings.

Working with a single informant in the Gabon in 1961 enabled ethnobotanists Walker and Sillan to publish a list of about 8,000 terms for local species known to a dozen neighbouring tribes. In *The Savage Mind* Claude Lévi-Strauss shows how supposedly ignorant tribal people amazed Western anthropologists with the depth of their knowledge of the surrounding fauna and flora. Among many others he quotes E. Smith Bowen's astonished first encounter with the botanical abilities of an African tribe:

> I found myself in a place where every man, woman and child knew literally hundreds of plants....

and Barrow among the American Indians:

> Several thousand Coahila Indians never exhausted the

143

natural resources of a desert region in South California, in which today only a handful of white families manage to subsist. They lived in a land of plenty, for in this apparently completely barren territory, they were familiar with no less than sixty kinds of edible plants and twenty-eight others of narcotic, stimulant or medicinal properties.

Lévi-Strauss was prompted to conclude:

Their extreme familiarity with their biological environment, the passionate attention which they pay to it and their precise knowledge of it has often struck inquirers as an indication of attitudes and preoccupations which distinguish the natives from their white visitors....

A thorough understanding of nature leads to a sensible and sustainable attitude towards the use of its resources. Early people were keen conservationists, although their societies relied more on taboos to maintain respect for the eco-systems, while we look to the findings of science to persuade the world to adopt modern 'green' practices. Our science is based on the concept of universal causality, the distinction between the subjective and the objective, and the view of time and space as infinite, continuous and homogenous. Our predecessors did not, however, distinguish between the subjective and the objective; causality for them was dependent on will; and their ideas of time and space were qualitative and concrete rather than quantitative and abstract.

In their version of the Garden of Eden myth, the Yao people of Malawi believed that God originally dwelt on earth with men. Then men learned how to make fire by friction; they set the grasslands alight and God withdrew into Heaven. According to the Bambuti of Central Africa, when God left them Death came instead, and they lost their happiness. The concrete realities are God, who goes; Death, which comes, and happiness which is lost. Burning the grasslands is a gross crime.

Colonialism and the Environment

Colonialism upset this harmonious relationship between African tribal people and nature by imposing ever-increasing demands on natural resources. It introduced large-scale agriculture, usually based on monoculture, and began massive deforestation. Intensive mining operations began, too, as colonialism ushered Africa into the era of resource-intensive 'development'.

The triangular relationship between people, economy and environment in Africa is more direct than in developed countries, where it is masked by technology. The cumulative effect of land-misuse, deforestation, drought, salination, pollution and desertification has reduced productivity and is the major cause behind the rampant poverty in Africa.

The gap between Africa and the industrialized capitalist countries (ICCs) is the fundamental product of world imperialism, which

> simultaneously generated the deepening crisis of underdevelopment in Africa. The concurrence of both development and underdevelopment on a global scale is the direct and systematic consequence of the differing effects of slavery, colonialism and neocolonialism on the ICCs, which reaped the advantages of these processes, and on Africa, which paid the price and bore the losses.[1]

The African mining industry is dominated by multinational corporations which invest very little in economic or environmental recovery. Huge intractable wastes encroach into life-support systems. Land reclamation is completely inappropriate.[2]

The USA, Western Europe and Japan depend on Africa for more than 50 per cent of their imports of bauxite, natural gas, phosphates, cobalt, uranium ore, alumina, chromium, manganese and other minerals. Yet very little hard information about the actual returns of these operations is forthcoming from the intricate web of the multinationals' corporate practice.

Post-colonialism — More of the Same

The newly independent African countries followed the patterns of economic development established during the period of direct colonialism. To bridge the gap between developed and developing countries it was considered essential to intensify the exploitation of natural resources and to concentrate industries — and their employees — in urban-industrial enclaves. Natural resources and the capacity of the environment to sustain pollutants were both tacitly assumed to be limitless.

The ecological degradation that followed 'development' hit the rural people hardest. The relative harshness of rural life drove millions into the 'prosperous' towns. The dilemma is that these towns depend to a large extent on rural products for export, raw materials and feeding their swollen populations.

Many policy-makers in Africa regarded industrialization as synonymous with development. The rush for industrialization, like the rush for gold, saw only the goal, not the way to it. The result is an economic and social liability, patchy, amateurish and unviable. And as Onimode has correctly remarked, 'Africa is implementing neither the capitalist, the socialist nor a systematic African mode of industrialization.'

Table 1. The Changing Pattern of World Grain Trade, 1950–88

Region	1950	1960	1970	1980	1988
	Million metric tonnes				
North America	+23	+39	+56	+131	+119
Latin America	+1	0	+4	−10	−11
Western Europe	−22	−25	−30	−16	+22
E. Europe & Soviet Union	0	0	0	−46	−27
Africa	0	−2	−5	−15	−28
Asia	−6	−17	−37	−63	−89
Australia & New Zealand	+3	+6	+12	+19	+14

Source: Lester R. Brown, *The State of the World*, (1990), World Watch Institute, p. 45.

Another problem is that developing countries are investing more in heavy industries, traditionally the most polluting, while the share of industries involved in food products has fallen significantly.[3] The result can be observed in the changing patterns of the world grain trade (Table 1).

Environmental Degradation

The land has suffered gross and rampant misuses. Vast stretches of forest were felled without replacement; Eastern Sudan and Western Ethiopia have seen 95 per cent of their woodland destroyed in the last century. Intensive and mechanized farming brings with it dependence on monoculture cash crops and the excessive use of agro-chemicals (pesticides and fertilizers), while giant projects for dams, canals and mining have gone ahead with little real consideration of their ecological impact. 'Modern Africa' has destroyed so much of the habitat, the wild-life and the flora, that the whole complex natural equilibrium has been upset; and it is the rural people, whose dependence on nature is most immediate, who suffer most acutely.

Tropical forests are shrinking by 11 million hectares a year. Topsoil is being lost at a rate of 26 billion tons a year. New deserts are appearing at the rate of 6 million hectares a year. Tropical developing countries have seen 160 million hectares of upland watershed grossly degraded over the last three decades. The *State of the World Population 1988* also reports that in many areas groundwater is being used faster than it is being replenished and that salination or waterlogging affect half the world's irrigated croplands.[4]

In many Sub-Saharan African countries the population has quadrupled in the last 50 years. In the same span of time 65 million hectares of land have been turned into desert, and the combined 'scissors effect' of poverty and increasing population has cut a bloody and tragic path.

Economic Degradation

The same rural people have suffered as a result of falling prices for agricultural products on the international market. Their real incomes have shrunk year after year. They gained nothing from the huge amounts of money borrowed by their governments in an attempt to sustain a false model of development. Instead, when repayment of these loans came due, the already meagre social services in rural areas were 'structured off'. Health and education services deteriorated very rapidly, while the onslaught on natural resources and life-support systems intensified.

Those who had not benefitted at all from the borrowing were obliged to shoulder the burden of repayment, with disastrous consequences for themselves and their environment.

By the end of the 1970s, 22 of the world's 31 least developed countries by UN classification were in Africa. In the 1980s some half a dozen African economies have collapsed, 15 are currently on the verge of disintegration, and almost all the rest are grinding to a halt.

The Changing Pattern of Rural—Urban Disparities

The rural—urban disparities, at first mainly cultural and social, have become increasingly economic and ecological. Statistical averages conceal the huge gap of rural—urban injustice. Even when the peasants and pastoralists flee to the towns, they are there obliged to live in enclaves and find themselves in conditions similar or worse than those they were trying to escape from.

Migrants flock to the cities hoping to find better access to social services and jobs. By the year 2000, 42 per cent of Africa's population will be urbanized, pushed to the cities by rural poverty. One cause of poverty is environmental degradation. It is estimated that between 1980 and 1985 at least 10 million

Africans were forced off their lands, largely by prolonged drought. They ended up in urban squatter camps or in refugee camps.

Many migrants find themselves in an economic trap. They work 10—15 hours a day for mere survival. One in four of their children die before the age of five. Half the adults suffer from intestinal worms and serious respiratory infections. According to the *State of the World Population 1988*, tuberculosis is increasing among the urban poor, as are AIDS and various other indications of social stress. Domestic abuse, rape and drug use are spreading.

Water for drinking and sanitation is scarce in many urban squatter settlements. It is not the quality of water that bothers squatters, but the quantity. WHO calculates that by 1983 only 39 per cent of the rural population in 92 countries had access to safe drinking water, compared to 72 per cent of the urban population. The latest statistics show that 3 billion people in developing countries still live without adequate sanitation and that more than 1.75 billion people have no access to a safe source of water.[5]

The debt service ratio (i.e., debt service payments as a percentage of annual export earnings) which was only 15 per cent in 1980, rose to over 50 per cent in 1987 for Sub-Saharan Africa, with 62 per cent for Ghana, 84 per cent for Equatorial Guinea and 204.6 per cent for Mozambique. For the 29 low-income Sub-Saharan countries, at the end of 1985, debt represented 425.5 per cent of annual export earnings and 80 per cent of GNP ... about twice the level of indebtedness of developing countries as a whole.

To illustrate the crisis situation, this year (1990), the Nigerian government estimated the total projected foreign exchange earnings through the public and private sector at $7.789 billion. From this amount defence and security affairs have been allocated $2.294 billion, while debt servicing takes $2.114 billion, which together is 56 per cent of the revenue.[6] (The net wealth transfer from developing countries increased from $10.2

billion in 1984 to $50.1 billion in 1988!)

Table 2 shows the debt profile for Nigeria from 1960 to 1987. A 65-fold increase in the last decade!

Table 2. Nigeria's External Debt Profile, 1960—87

Year	Total debt (N million)
1960	82.4
1965	435.2
1970	448.8
1977	1,008.8
1978	1,988.8
1981	12,800.0
1982	14,742.0
1983	17,758.0
1984	21,385.0
1985	21,200.0
1986	35,060.0
1987	65,000.0

Note: 1987 is an approximation. As a conversion from dollar to *naira* value under the Second-Tier Foreign Exchange Market (SFEM), this is actually an understatement. The World Bank's *World Development Report* (1986) puts the external debt figure for 1986 at US$22.7 billion. At the N4.00 to US$1.00 SFEM rate, this translates to N90.8 billion.

Source: Business Concord, 21 May 1986 (Lagos), quoted from Bade Onimode (ed.), *IMF, World Bank and African Debt* (London, Zed Books, 1989), p. 159.

Food First

To remedy the injustice, and to put poor African countries on the path to economic and environmental rehabilitation and recovery, most aid, most efforts and most facilities should go to rural people and rural development, with the primary objective of producing food. The objective of producing cash crops must be placed second. A successful return to the villages can only be attained when the quality of life in the rural countryside is better than in the squalid shanty-towns.

In many African countries farm prices are subsidized to provide the trouble-makers in the cities with cheap food. Small farmers have no incentive to increase food production. They also have no surplus cash to invest in soil conservation, fertilizers, better seeds or machinery. Besides, the prices for export cash crops have dropped over the past decade.

Equally alarming is the fact that the patterns of land use which sustained many generations of rural Africans have been broken. Increase in population and decrease in rainfall push people to exploit marginal land, shorten fallow periods and clear more land, thus reducing fuelwood supplies and grazing land. Finally, the topsoil itself turns into dust.

The *State of the World Population 1988* gives several examples of successful rural development programmes built on community action. We cite two here:

- Kenya's national soil conservation programme is generally regarded as one of the most successful in Africa. The programme began in 1974 and by 1984 Kenyans — mostly women — had terraced 365,000 farms, or two out of every five.
- Similarly, Zimbabwe's 'maize miracle' was the result of a concerted national programme to build up the productivity of small-scale farmers, again mostly women. The results were impressive: maize yields doubled, reaching 2.5–4 metric tonnes per hectare in the mid-1980s.

The Role of African Women in Development

Eighty-eight per cent of rural African women work in agriculture. They produce, process and market 80 per cent of the food. In addition to child-rearing, providing health care for the family and running the household, women spend the equivalent of an eight-hour day job transporting water, fuel and goods. Women also run 70 per cent of all micro-enterprises in developing countries, and yet they have another duty to fulfil: that of resource manager. They do whatever environmental protection work is possible — for example, in soil conservation.

The central role of women in resource use, conservation and rehabilitation has been overlooked by governments and international agencies. As sustainable development policies take hold, so the responsibilities of women in conservation and rehabilitation of natural resources will increase. It should be emphasized in this context that sustainable development policies can only succeed if they take this central role of women into full consideration.

Sustainable development policies should aim at releasing women from some of their burdens and at giving them access to education, training and health care. This will raise their stature as human personalities and allow them to participate more fully in political, cultural and social spheres, endowing them with the will and perspectives to change their lives, society and the environment. There is a powerful truth in the words of Phoebe Asiyo: 'The dreams of women are the dreams of their nations'.

The inability of African governments, women's organizations, NGOs and so on to ensure the full participation of rural women in political, economic and cultural activities is a major setback to development, environmental conservation and social progress in Africa. These deprived women hold the riches of the future in their hands.

Free Market — Free to Destroy?

Economic and environmental rehabilitation demands stricter measures against the forces of the international 'free market' economy, which in the conditions of poor developing countries leads to destructive, often irreversible exploitation of natural resources, does incalculable harm to life-support systems and social and economic infrastructures, and forces shattering poverty on millions upon millions of people, particularly in rural areas and suburban shanty-towns.

The industrialized countries contain less than 25 per cent of the world's population, but they consume 75 per cent of the world's energy output, 79 per cent of all commercial fuels, 85 per cent of all wood production and 72 per cent of steel production.

Development as an ideology allows the indirect entry of global market domination. It creates a need for international aid and foreign debt which provide the capital for such development projects that commercialise or privatise resources. Control over local resources thus increasingly shifts out of the hands of local communities and even national governments into the hands of international financial institutions. The conditions for loans determine the mode or utilization of natural resources. The pressure of repayment and servicing of debts further consolidates the globalization. Total integration with the global market economy thus marginalizes the concern for the economy of natural processes and the survival economy. In the resulting anarchy of resource use, the visible enclaves of economic development with their élite minority residents get disproportionately high access to resources, while the invisible hinterlands of economic under-development — the homes of the silent majority — are left with shrinking access to a shrinking resource base.[7]

Even the President of the World Bank acknowledges that prospects for the poor are bleak.

Some studies of global warming predict simultaneous crop failures in all those regions now considered the bread baskets of the world, and the poor would be the hardest hit because they have the least resources to adapt to change.[8]

Profit-oriented market forces respect only the cash value of things and pay no regard to the real value of natural resources and human beings. Making profit at the expense of the latter is both justified and actively pursued by free market operators, whether indigenous or international, who divert natural wealth from the people to the market for their own gain. As American Indian leader Chief Seattle saw in 1854, when he was offered a reservation in exchange for a large area of Indian land:

How can you buy or sell the sky, the warmth of the land? The idea is strange to us. If we do not own the freshness of the air and the sparkle of the water, how can you buy them? ... We know that the white man does not understand our ways. One portion of land is the same to him as the next, for he is a stranger who comes in the night and takes from the land whatever he needs. The earth is not his brother but his enemy, and when he has conquered it, he moves on.... He treats his mother, the earth, and his brother, the sky, as things to be bought, plundered, sold like sheep or bright beads. His appetite will devour the earth and leave behind only a desert....

Teach your children what we have taught our children, that the earth is our mother. Whatever befalls the earth befalls the sons of the earth. If men spit upon the ground, they spit upon themselves. This we know: the earth does not belong to man, man belongs to the earth. All things are connected like the blood which unites one family. Whatever befalls the earth befalls the sons of the earth. Man did not weave the web of life: he is merely a strand in it. Whatever he does to the web, he does to himself.... This earth is precious to him, and to harm the earth is to heap contempt on its Creator. The whites too shall pass: perhaps sooner than all other tribes. Contaminate your bed, and you will one night suffocate in your own waste. But in your perishing you will shine brightly, fired by the strength of the God who brought you to this land and for some special purpose gave you dominion over this land and over the red man. That destiny is a mystery to us, for we do not understand when the buffalo are all slaughtered, the wild horses are tamed, the secret corners of the forest heavy with the scent of many men, and the view of the ripe

hills blotted by talking wires.
Where is the thicket? Gone. Where is the eagle? Gone.
The end of living and the beginning of survival.
(GAIA Peace Atlas (1988) Pan Books).

Basic Needs — People's Needs

Poor developing countries must evolve a new system of project evaluation, one that is holistic and forward-looking. Every development project should satisfy people's real economic, social and environmental needs. The poor should benefit from positive discrimination, to redress the negative discrimination they have been experiencing for so many decades.

> The present emergency in Africa [is] not ... a short-term crisis brought on by any one exceptional circumstance but ... a surfacing of a long-term crisis of poverty and underdevelopment ... nearly four million African children [die] each and every year — even when there is no drought, no famine, no camps, no epidemics and no media coverage.[9]

Now that the socialist countries are going through difficult times and the Third World countries are tamed at last by the whip of debt, developed capitalist countries are enjoying unmitigated power over most of the world. This spells danger for developing countries and, in the end, danger for those capitalist countries themselves. The pursuit of profit can pressurize developing countries to extract the last drop of their dwindling resources, so that regional and international conflicts may become unavoidable. Environmental conflict may grow from local skirmishes over grazing and water into prolonged wars.

Holistic development must ensure the means of survival, food, water and shelter before advancing to higher aspirations. An approach to the environment as a unified, diverse totality must seek to open the eyes of those who destroy the environment without a pang of conscience or fear because they are distanced from the effect of their actions. A holistic approach does not only mean looking at all aspects of the issue at stake, but also means getting the priorities right. The top priority in Africa now is the need of rural people — especially women — for the means of survival.

The agrarian malaise of Africa lies not only in decreasing food production but extends to the export sector, where Africa's share of world trade in commodities like coffee, tea and sugar has declined. Progress in research in biotechnology could further undermine exports. Falling export earnings go on to hit the industrial sector and social services, and lead to further debts. At the same time Africa's food imports are increasing rapidly (Table 3). In the 1960s, the volume of grain imports doubled and total costs rose by 50 per cent. During the 1970s, grain imports rose by 100 per cent, and many African countries could not pay for essential imports.

Table 3. The Growth of Sub-Saharan Africa's Food Imports, 1961–82

Commodity	Average annual change in volume (%)		Average annual value (US$m)		
	1961/63–1969/71	1969/71–1980/82	1961/63	1969/71	1980/82
Rice	4.9	12.4	63	91	961
Wheat	12.9	10.9	30	81	648
Maize	8.7	14.4	12	32	381
Other cereals	8.7	0.2	9	21	58
Cereals total	9.0	12.7	114	225	2,321
Dairy products	7.2	—	44	109	670
Sugar	2.5	6.5	84	109	836
Meat	1.3	10.7	20	24	267
Animal/vegetable oils	10.3	14.9	20	48	465
Total for Sub-Saharan Africa:	4.3	—	749	1,137	6,833
Total for oil exporters:	1.5	—	151	207	2,738
Total for others:	5.1	—	598	930	4,095

Source: World Bank, *Towards Sustained Development in Sub-Saharan Africa* (1984).

The Impact of the Greenhouse Effect

Climatologists predict a relatively small increase in average temparatures in the tropics; perhaps 1 degree Celsius by the middle of next century. Farming in the tropics is, however, more vulnerable to small variations in the weather than is the case in other regions. Moisture also plays a crucial role in the survival of crops and natural vegetation. A minor change in the distribution of rainfall, or a change in the timing of seasonal rains, might have disastrous repercussions on agriculture and might lead to drought or floods. Major food shortages would result. It is therefore a legitimate question whether impoverished African countries with a growing malnourished population would be in a position to rectify the severe repercussions of far-reaching climatic changes. Hunger might trigger mass population movement. Tribal, ethnic and regional conflicts might become endemic.

Already the growth of food/cash crop production is destroying the land and water resources on which future output depends. The Food and Agricultural Organization (FAO) estimates that without conservation measures soil degradation and erosion will destroy — by the year 2100 — 65 per cent of the croplands which depend on rainfall in Africa.

The Worldwatch Institute underlined the message in its *State of the World 1988* report:

To continue with a more or less business-as-usual attitude — to accept the loss of tree cover, erosion of soil, the expansion of deserts, the loss of plant and animal species, the depletion of the ozone layer, and the build-up of greenhouse gases — implies acceptance of economic decline and social disintegration. In a world where progress depends on a complex set of national and international economic ties, such disintegration would bring human suffering on a scale that has no precedent. The threat now posed by continuing environmental deterioration is no longer a hypothetical one. Dozens of countries will have lower living standards at the end of the 1980s than at the beginning. We can no longer assume that economic progress is automatic anywhere.

Civil Wars

Civil wars in Africa have caused immeasurable losses in terms of human lives, the environment and the social fabric and stability of many nations. The major cause of most civil wars is economic poverty. The tragic dilemma is that wars destroy the productive land, the forests, the animals, the fresh water, the mineral and energy resources — and thereby exacerbate the poverty and deepen the root cause of conflict. Environmental degradation also degrades the people and is increasingly becoming a factor in civil wars and ethnic riots. As noted above, the impact on the environment of major climatic changes could be the beginning of further social upheavals. Understanding the link between poverty, degradation of resources and civil and ethnic conflicts is a prerequisite for peace in Africa.

Population Growth Depletes Resources

The world population — now 5 billion — will be 6 billion by the end of the century. Nearly all this growth is in the developing countries, those least capable of absorbing it. The growth of population, the depletion of natural resources and the drop in price of export commodities constitute a triangle of despair. For many of the rural poor, all that can be hoped for now is sheer survival — the dream of development and social progress must be abandoned.

The agenda for change postulated by the United Nations Population Fund (UNPF) lies in an integrated policy response for population and resource management. People and nature can be saved, but only when we restore a healthy equilibrium to our ecosystem. It has to be stated clearly that there is no single population recipe valid for all countries. We have to remember that economic development took place in the now industrialized countries in the context of high rates of population growth, and that in some developing countries food shortages, malaria and AIDS constitute a three-dimensional death trap. There are perhaps as many population problems as there are countries, but the trend is global.

Technologies for Sustainable Development

Technology, we are told, will generate development and wealth: hence it is the only way to environmental rehabilitation. The fallacy that technology has magic solutions for every problem stems from the one-sided attitude that since technology *per se* is the driving force in developed countries, it must be the same everywhere else. But technological development has in many cases caused environmental degradation and severe depletion of natural reserves, as well as poisoning our air, water and food, to say nothing of its effect on societal structures.

> With each passing day its potential for bringing about swift and widespread amelioration of man is only matched by its potential for even swifter and more widespread damage and destruction of man and his environment.[10]

The social and ecological cost of many 'viable' technologies is high. Their productivity in a market-oriented economy is usually at the cost of non-renewable natural resources. Developed countries with efficient technologies are siphoning off our common wealth: our common future is being consumed *now*! Profit maximization in developed countries generates poverty maximization in developing countries. This is why developing countries need sustainable technologies, that is, technologies efficient in production that do not make too heavy a demand on natural resources and human beings.

Developing countries do not need, and cannot afford, to adopt technology indiscriminately. They need appropriate, sustainable technologies that do not over-consume or rely heavily on natural resources. In developed countries the spatial separation between where reserves are being exhausted and where commodities are being produced has masked the devastation of resources that is taking place in the developing countries. Gandhi foresaw the danger implicit in resource-intensive technologies:

> God forbid that India should ever take to industrialism after the manner of the West. The economic imperialism of a single tiny island kingdom (England) is today keeping the world in chains. If an entire nation of 300 million took to a similar economic exploitation, it would strip the world bare like locusts.[11]

Classic Development, Classic Failure

The ideology of classic economic development, based on a preoccupation with growth, has continued to fail in many African countries. It has brought economic and ecological crisis and has been unable to solve the problem of abject poverty. Alternative strategies should rely on indigenous renewable resources, should be geared to satisfy the needs of the indigenous people, and should elicit and rely on their participation and cooperation. Alternative strategies must enhance the quality of life for the largest number of people and abandon the preoccupation with the material standard of living of an élite few.

Pursuing growth, many African countries have ended up in debt. To repay that debt, the exploitation of natural resources and human beings has been intensified. Forests, grazing and farm lands are being destroyed, and with them the people and the natural fauna and flora. But even if all debts were cancelled now, the destruction would continue as long as 'economic' growth and not the quality of life is the sole aim of development strategies. As 'structural adjustment' budgets bite, even education ceases to be a basic priority.

> I studied here when I was younger. It was a wonderful school, the best secondary school in the North. But now we can't keep it up. The small budget I have is only enough for light bulbs and stationary supplies for the office. It is falling apart. There are many things that need to be done. If we do not do minor repairs now, they become major repairs and much harder to tackle.[12]

Return to Positive Cultural Values

A strong element in the conservation of the environment and the improvement of the quality of life of the African people is the preservation of indigenous cultural values. We should be proud of our excellent social and cultural traditions in housing, clothes and food; in self-help, cooperation and solidarity.

A true return to positive traditional values does not entail a nostalgic view of the past, nor an attempt to re-run it. On the contrary, it means catering for real human needs using local materials, tools and manpower. It is self-reliance and cooperation versus consumerism and imported luxury. Many of our staple foods, abandoned by city dwellers, could easily be sold in Europe as health foods!

> After the war I called *nafeer* (community action meeting) and together with relatives and friends I built this house with mud bricks. In the 1960s we thought that the living room was not good enough, so we pulled it down and built a larger one with concrete and all. But it was hot so we saved and bought a cooler. Now we do not use it any longer because when electricity is there, the water is cut, and when water is there the electricity is cut. I cannot afford to pull it down and I can now only use it in winter.[13]

Amalgamating Modern and Indigenous Education

Everywhere in Africa modern general school education is replacing the traditional indigenous educational systems, rather than supplementing them. The result is literate people who may know how to read books but do not know the ways of nature; people who are alien in their own surroundings, unable to maintain a harmonious relationship with the fauna and flora around them, to respect the balance of give and take.

To obtain a modern education, rural children move to rural towns and from there to big towns and cities. By the time they have 'made it' to higher secondary school or college, they are so far up the social ladder that they do not want to go back to their villages. They will also be so far educated out of their indigenous traditional culture that they no longer know how to live in nature, with nature, off nature.

An amalgamation of the two educational systems, the modern and the traditional, is an important step towards sustained economic, cultural and social development.

The reaction of a specialist to indigenous education is quite different. In a monograph in which he describes nearly three hundred species or varieties of medicinal or toxic plants used by certain peoples of [Zambia], Gilges writes: 'It has always been a surprise to me to find with what eagerness the people in and around Balovale were ready and willing to talk about their medicines. Was it that they found my interest in their methods pleasing? Was it an exchange of information amongst colleagues? Or was it to show off their knowledge? Whatever the reason, information was readily forthcoming. I remember a wicked old Luchozi who brought bundles of dried leaves, roots and stems and told me about their uses. How far he was a herbalist and how far a witch-doctor I could never fathom, but I regret that I shall never possess his knowledge of African psychology and his art in the treatment of his fellow men that, coupled with my scientific medical knowledge, might have made a most useful combination....[14]

People's Participation —
the Prerequisite for Development

The shortcomings in economic and social performances in Africa over the last decade are the result not only of misguided approaches to development but also of institutional crisis. The Western-style, state-centred legal, legislative and executive institutions have rapidly become a burden to progress. The almost total reliance on the state for development and social change is a direct consequence of the destruction of the traditional values of tribal democracy, cooperation, self-reliance and solidarity. Relaxing state control in favour of traditional local self-government is therefore one of the prerequisites for positive change.

Self-government and self-reliance should in no way encourage isolationist tendencies on the part of nations or local communities. On the contrary, they should be understood as:

a process capable of promoting participation in decision-making, social creativity, political self-determination, a fair distribution of wealth and tolerance for the diversity of identities. Self-reliance becomes a turning point in the articulation of human beings with nature and technology, of the personal with the social, of the micro with the macro, of autonomy with planning, and of civil society with the state.[15]

The ECA's formulation of the role of participation in development will be much quoted:

It should be emphasized that the urgency of alleviating mass poverty and of increasing the welfare of the African people is rooted not simply in the humanistic or altruistic aspects of development. It is predicated, above all, on the rational proposition that development has to be engineered and sustained by the people themselves through their full and active participation. Development should not be undertaken on behalf of a people; rather it should be the organic outcome of a society's value system, its percept-ions, its concerns and its endeavours. As such, to achieve and sustain development, it is necessary to ensure the education and training, health, well-being and vitality of the people so that they can participate fully and effectively in the development process.[16]

The African Alternative

The alternative strategy for African countries should:

1   satisfy the basic needs of the majority of people;
2   improve the quality of their lives;
3   conserve and rehabilitate the environment in which they live; and
4   ensure a just and equitable distribution of national wealth.

We see the following measures as necessary and practical for the implementation of an alternative strategy:

1   people's participation, which can be achieved only among free people in a free society;
2   looking inward, which entails self-reliance, a return to tradi-tional cultural and social values, the use of indigenous materials and local manpower;
3   cooperation: macro-cooperation on national, regional and continental levels; micro-cooperation at cooperative and self-help levels; and

Above all, the African alternative will recognize the need for a deeper understanding of the triangular interdependency, especially in the Third World, of sustainable development, peace and democracy. These three things seem to rise or fall together.

NOTES

1 Bade Onimode, *A Political Economy of the African Crisis*, Zed Books (1988), p. 20.
2 Minewatch Briefings, 1-10.
3 UN World Commission on the Environment and Development, *Our Common Future* (1987).
4 UN Population Fund, *State of the World Population, 1988/*
5 United Nations Development Programme (UNDP), *Human Development Report 1990.*
6 *National Concord,* 12 March 1990.
7 Bandyopadhyay and Shiva, *Political Economy of Ecology Movements* (IFDA Dossier 71), p. 56.
8 B. Conable, World Bank President, quoted in *Spur,* October 1989.
9 James Grant, Director, United Nations Children's Fund (UNICEF).
10 *Development Dialogue* (1988), Vol 1–2, p. 6.
11 M. K. Gandhi, *Young India* (1928), p. 42.
12 Interview with Manuel Gabriel, Director of Nampula Secondary School, Mozambique, July 1988.
13 From an interview with a Sudanese in Omdurman by F. B. Mahmoud, whose *Housing Strategies in the Sudan* is forthcoming.
14 Claude Lévi-Strauss, *The Savage Mind,* p. 6.
15 'Human scale development', in *Development Dialogue* (1989), Vol. 1, p. 49.
16 ECA, *AAF–SAP,* p. 11.

Self-Reliance and Popular Participation

Dr Omar Ali Juma

Your conference has been meeting at a very significant time in the world's history. With the independence of Namibia an end to direct colonialism in Africa seems to approach. We can now see that the time is not far away when the people of South Africa will completely eradicate racism and apartheid in their beloved country.

We also hope that the people of Western Sahara will soon be given the opportunity to exercise their right to self-determination and independence.

With Africa now almost free from colonial tutelage, it is apt that we should concentrate our attention on the discussion of economic development, cultural regeneration and advances in science and technology. Thirty years of independence have been used mostly by interests hostile to Africa's advancement. We have seen how some leaders, consciously or unconsciously, have engaged themselves as pawns of extra-colonial powers; how African economies have been compromised to remain as appendages of the metropole; and how cultural values and beliefs have been discarded in favour of a 'coco-cola culture'.

Africa is a continent bigger in size than the whole of Western Europe and Japan combined. Historically this continent used to produce more than enough food for itself and for export. Yet now, with the exception of very few countries, Africa depends on food handouts from the developed countries. The fertile lands of Angola, the highlands of Kenya, the untapped areas of Zambia, Zaire and Sudan can produce food in abundance to feed the whole continent and for export. There is no reason why every year hundreds of Africans should die of hunger. Even with the desertification and the drought seen in the Sahel and Ethiopia, or the man-made disasters such as that inflicted on Mozambique, one still cannot explain why there should be starvation on this continent. In this last decade of the twentieth century, Africa has to take seriously the fact that food is politics, and that the one who gives you food aid determines (to a certain extent) your political destiny. We have seen, in the last thirty years, how a lack of seriousness on the part of some of our countries in tackling the food problems has exposed them to various political machinations. Haven't we seen how African governments have been forced to vote in certain ways at international fora in order to receive food assistance? It is in this context that Zanzibar has embarked on a nation-wide campaign for food self-sufficiency through more intensive agriculture and improved methods of farming.

Although Africa contains 7.5 per cent of the world's population, it accounts for only 1.2 per cent of the global GNP, 1.6 per cent of the world's export earnings, and only 1.1 per cent of the total world public expenditure on health.

Our continent has the highest rate of infant mortality, and hundreds and thousands of children die every year of measles, whooping cough, tetanus, diptheria and other preventable diseases. This situation will continue for years to come unless a radical re-orientation takes place and the continent evolves and implements different development strategies from those that have been followed so far. It is my sincere hope that the conference had wide deliberations on this and came up with viable suggestions for our governments to consider.

Thirty years of independence have also brought in dictatorships and tyrannical regimes in some African countries. We have seen how in some of these countries, and not just in white-ruled South Africa, elementary democratic rights have been trampled upon and basic human rights recognized by all civilized mankind have been denied to millions of our people.

We have seen the killings and torture of the Amins, the Bokassas and their like. Whatever the strategies formulated by our governments for our peoples in the economic and social spheres, therefore, they must be coupled with strategies in the political arena. Mobilization of the people to take an active part in their own development and that of their country has always been the focal point of Tanzania's development policies.

After thirty years of independence, Africa appears to be more dependent on foreign aid than ever before. There is no major project of either national or regional significance that has been conceived and implemented in Africa without foreign support. In fact, quite often, even minor projects depend entirely on donor support, to the extent that in some places the people get the impression that African governments have abandoned their responsibilities in development and delegated them to foreign governments and donor agencies.

Africa's problems have been compounded recently with the increase of debt. Africa has the highest proportion of debt to GNP. The total debt of the countries of sub-Saharan Africa (excluding South Africa) represents more than 75 per cent of the countries' GNP and 350 per cent of their exports. Between 1980 and 1984, these countries' debt service payments (including payments to the IMF) increased from 18 per cent of export earnings to 20 per cent. The ratio of countries like Malawi, Niger and Zambia rose to more than 30 per cent. Notwithstanding the fact that about 70 per cent of the debt is with governments and multilateral institutions like the IMF and the World Bank, this debt burden is crushing.

Interest and ammortization charges have soared from $8 billion in 1985 to $19.5 billion in 1987 and to over $25 billion in 1988. The net payment by Africa to IMF alone was $1 billion by 1986.

Studies on the debt problem in many countries have revealed the use of millions and millions of dollars, acquired through loans, on luxury and superfluous goods; on travel abroad or on personal deposits and investments in foreign banks. All governments and private companies borrow in response to unavoidable needs at given times. But they do so in the belief that once the need is met, the borrowing will cease. However, foreign indebtedness in Africa has become an addiction; the dose is increasing everyday.

One cannot but agree with the Executive Secretary of the Economic Commission for Africa, Professor Adebayo Adedeji, that Africa, more than any other Third World region, is faced with a development crisis of great portent. But what are the solutions?

The so-called solutions being offered to the developing countries by the international financial institutions are not solutions at all: sometimes they are part of the problem. Their programmes, such as 'partners for progress', 'structural adjustment', 'adjustment with a human face' and so on can only be palliatives. The pain returns even more forcefully once the effect of the analgesic wears off.

I know in your three-day deliberations you have looked at different options and discussed a number of alternatives available to our countries. But any option and any alternative development strategy must involve all the social forces, from its inception to its implementation, and must include public discussions and debates at all its stages. To attempt otherwise is to invite failure, and to continue to be condemned to underdevelopment.

I also hope that you have had an opportunity, even if a digressional one, to analyze the current events in Eastern Europe. There are probably a number of lessons we can draw from them, including certainly the need for a high degree of openness in dealing with socio-political developments and the full involvement of the people to withstand capitalist pressures. We can not affort to sit idle while a full rapprochement between the East and West develops. This rapprochement has a number of implications for us. Seemingly the most obvious is the likelihood of Western countries redirecting their resources and attention to the East. Being geographically nearer to Western

Europe and having a well-developed economic infrastructure, Eastern Bloc countries hold out the promise of quicker returns on investment than African countries do. And this is not to mention the political determination of the West to prove what they profess is the failure of communism.

Now more than ever before, African countries need to realize that their survival as independent nations lies in their own efforts to achieve self-reliance and actualization. At this juncture, we may wish to take note of President Fidel Castro's recent remarks that 'imperialism is inviting the socialist countries of Europe to become beneficiaries of its surplus capital, to develop capitalism themselves and take part in the looting of Third World nations'.

Index

64, 121, 122, 134
trade liberalization, 50, 53—4, 62, 63,
64, 121, 122, 134
trade unions, 61, 63, 68, 70, 79, 88,
106, 109, 112, 131
transport, 4, 9, 30, 64, 67

Uganda, 26, 42, 80, 84
underdevelopment, 45, 50, 94, 104,
109, 145, 153
United National Independence Party
(UNIP), 84
United States (US), 21, 22, 42, 46, 53,
54, 55, 56, 63, 72, 75, 89, 91, 145, 154
United Nations (UN), 7, 18, 20, 42, 43,
65, 127, 148; Convention on the
Elimination of All Forms of Dis-
crimination Against Women, 127;
Decade for Women, 127, 128, 129,
130; Fourth Development Decade
(1990s), 16, 44; International
Development Strategy, 16; Third
Development Decade (1980s), 16,
43; UN Declaration of Human
Rights, 75, 127; UN Development
Plan (UNDP), 47; UNICEF, 65; UN
Population Fund (UNPF), 158;
UNTAG, 75; see also ECA, FAO,
ILO, WHO
University of Dar es Salaam, 3
University of Lovanium, 85
University of Nairobi, 87

Villagization Programme, 123

water, 4, 30, 46, 67, 134, 149, 155, 157,
158, 159
Western Sahara, 169
Wollo, 27
women, 106, 107, 112, 127—39, 151,
152, 156; feminist movement, 130,
131, 135, 136, 138; Forward Looking
Strategies, 128, 129, 130; Nairobi
conference, 128; organizations,
128, 129, 130, 135, 136, 138, 152; UN
Decade for Women, 127, 128, 129,
130
World Bank, see IMF/World Bank
World Health Organization (WHO),
133, 149
Worldwatch Institute, 157; State of
the World 1988, 157

Yao, 144
Yoruba, 27, 72

Zaire, 84, 85, 169
Zambia, 51, 57, 83, 84, 87, 106, 162,
169, 171
Zanzibar, 170
Zimbabwe, 84, 151

INSTITUTE FOR AFRICAN ALTERNATIVES

DIRECTOR: Ben Turok BScEng,MILS,BA(SA),MA(DSM)

COUNCIL: Prof Bade Onimode (Nigeria) Chair
Prof Abdoulaye Bathily (Senegal)
Dr T Berhane-Selassie (Ethiopia)
Prof Fatima Babiker Mahmoud(Sudan)
Dr Kwame Ninsin (Ghana)
Prof Nzongola-Ntalaja (Zaire)

Prof B Magubane(South Africa)
Mr Kmepton Makamure(Zimbabwe)
Dr E Mwanang'onze (Zambia)
Prof Haroub Othman (Tanzania)

IFAA
23 Bevenden Street
London N1 6BH
UK

Phone 01 251 1503
Telex 923753W6019

IFAA was established in 1986 to promote policy research and discussion on the contemporary problems of Africa. Its headquarters are located in London, UK, and consists of a suite of offices, a lecture hall, a common room and study rooms. Facilities are available for visiting Research Fellows from Africa. A network of IFAA Resource Centres is being established in seven countries in Africa.

ACTIVITIES

Conferences, Workshops, Seminars:

A major annual conference is held at IFAA with invited speakers from across Africa. There is also a special conference on African women. Workshops are held on a specialist basis and seminars on particular topics. Proceedings are generally recorded and published.

Lectures and Classes

IFAA holds a series of lectures on particular topics from time to time. Classes are run on such topics as History of African Women, Problems of Development, Neocolonialism, South African Liberation etc. A residential three month course on African Women: Transformation and Development is under preparation.

IFAA is an INDEPENDENT CENTRE of the UNIVERSITY OF LONDON and runs joint Diploma and other courses with the Centre of Extramural Studies.

Publishing

IFAA publishes its conference proceedings, books by IFAA Associates, textbooks for African Universities, and occasional papers.

IFAA issues a bi-monthly newsletter **IFAA NEWS**, and a quarterly bibiliography of African books **IFAA BOOK LISTINGS**.

INSTITUTE FOR AFRICAN ALTERNATIVES

and
Institute of Development Studies (IDS)
University of Dar es Salaam

DAR ES SALAAM DECLARATION
'Alternative Development Strategies for Africa'

Adopted at the conference on
'Alternative Development Strategies'
held at the University of Dar es Salaam, 12-14 December 1989

Sponsored by Institute of Development Studies (IDS) University of Dar es Salaam
and Institute For African Alternatives (IFAA)

1. This conference representing the academic community, Churches, Labour, Women, Non-Governmental Organisations, Government Officials and students across Africa notes with alarm the deteriorating conditions all over the continent. There is a sharp decline in living standards for the great majority of the people, economies are faltering, education standards are falling steeply and social services are collapsing.

2. Conference condemns the policies imposed on African peoples, with or without the complicity of African governments, by multinational agencies such as the IMF and the World Bank which are enforced through harsh conditionalities tied to Funding in pursuance of Structural Adjustment or Economic Recovery Programmes. These bodies insist on massive payments for debt servicing beyond the capacities of debtor countries. We record our collective indignation at the continuing disregard of the massive destruction of African currencies and economies as well as the socio-political costs of these repressive measures.

3. We note that the members of the Group of Seven industrialised countries seem to be committed to the stance of the IMF and the World Bank and are probably the architects of their policies.

4. Hence Conference re-affirms IFAA's earlier call, that of OATUU (Organisation of African Trade Union Unity), and other social groups and institutions, on our governments to take concerted political action on foreign debt and form an **African Debtors Cartel** to match the creditor cartels and link up with Latin America and South-East Asia in a Third World Debtors' Cartel. The OAU's earlier decision to hold an international conference on foreign debt should also be implemented early in 1990. Conference also calls for a moratorium of ten years for all external debt repayments and the cancellation of all the debts or their conversion into grants. Failing these, African countries should collectively repudiate the external debts as unjust, immoral and oppressive.

5. Conference endorses IFAA's adoption of AAF-SAP (African Alternative Framework to Structural Adjustment Programmes for Socio-Economic Recovery and Transformation) as Africa's credible alternative to failed Economic Recovery or Structural Adjustment Programmes (SAP's or ERP's). Hence we call on our governments to scrap their IMF and World Bank SAP's or ERP's, currency auction, massive devaluations and flexible exchange rate systems and to replace them with alternative programmes based on AAP-SAP. The IMF, World Bank and the international community should respect the sovereignty of African countries by supporting these alternative programmes both technically and financially.

6. We note the historic parallels between the restructuring of the world economy in the 1940s and 1990s with emergent East-West detente, reforms in Eastern Europe and regional trading blocs in North America, Europe 1992 and Pacific Asia that are imposing involuntary de-linking on Africa. These challenges demand urgent steps by our governments and peoples to adopt **alternative development strategies.** These should aim at creating a new social order based on people-centred development, popular democracy and social justice on the basis of effective African Integration at sub-regional and regional levels as well as South-South Cooperation. This re-orientation of African development should focus on planned disengagement from international capitalism, regional food self-sufficiency, satisfaction of basic needs for all, development from below through the termination of anti-rural bias as well as concentration on relevant small and medium scale enterprises.

7. Alternative strategies in agriculture and rural development must empower the peasant majority, ensure access and control to agricultural inputs for all cultivators especially women and reorganise agriculture on a cooperative basis with increased investment for improved technology. Industrialisation should similarly be based mainly on domestic needs and local resources with selective joint manufaturing of intermediate and capital goods like fertilisers, steel, tractors, etc. The myth of technology transfer should also be replaced with indigneous development of technology through massive scientific and engineering institutions and production enterprises, increased funding of research tied to direct production as well as the standardisation of equipment and machinery.

8. Conference affirms that alternative development in Africa should see the current crisis as a political crisis linked to a basic contradiction between state power and people's power. This should be resolved through urgent democratisation of our countries with effective popular participation at all levels in decision-making and resource allocation on a basis of community empowerment. The basic role of the state in development through effective planning should be strengthened and made more efficient. This demands patriotic leadership and effective accountability without which there can be no development.

9. Our governments should coordinate and develop their capabilities with respect to information and personnel in the control of multinational corporations that have become major agents of decapitalisation in Africa. Joint investment codes for these multinationals should be established in order to coordinate the regulatory framework for these enterprises, especially on transfer pricing.

10. Conference maintains that alternative development must ensure women equity in the transformation process. Hence we support the declarations on women that establish specific targets for women by the year 2000 in top executive posts, general employment, and the elimination of discriminatory legislations. We call on our governments to implement these imaginative targets. This requires the mental decolonisation of men and women in a framework of democratic social development with equity and solidarity through networking among African women.

11. As the African environmental crisis is laden with emergent ecological problems, there is need for the technical study of Africa's environmental problems which are different from those of the North. The environmental impact of development projects should be assessed systematically and regulatory laws on the environment should be re-examined and implemented effectively. Dumping of all types of toxic waste from developed countries should be strictly prohibited.

12. The Conference follows with admiration and hope the unfolding of the liberation process especially in Southern Africa. We urge all African peoples and governments to support actively the fight against colonialism and apartheid.

13. Conference notes that the most basic problem with alternative development strategies in Africa is their implementation. This requires that development documents in Africa must become political documents that should be widely disseminated and debated. Then the popular forces of workers, peasants, women, students, progressive intellectuals as well as patriotic professionals and politicians have to be mobilised for the implementation of alternative development so that Africa can turn the lost decade of the 1980s into a launching pad for its rapid recovery and transformation from the 1990s.

IFAA, 23 Bevenden Street, London N1 6BH, UK

Telephone: 071-251 1503   Telex: 262433 MONREF GW6019   Fax: 071-490 4070